NO LONGER PROPERTY OF
NO LONGER PROPERTY OF
SEATTLE PUBLIC LIBRARY

OVER THE TOP

OVER THE TOP

A Raw Journey to Self-Love

JONATHAN VAN NESS

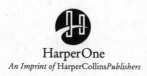

HarperOne

An Imprint of HarperCollinsPublishers

HarperOne

OVER THE TOP. Copyright © 2019 by Jonathan Van Ness. All rights reserved. Printed in the United States of America. No part of this book may be used or reproduced in any manner whatsoever without written permission except in the case of brief quotations embodied in critical articles and reviews. For information, address HarperCollins Publishers, 195 Broadway, New York, NY 10007.

HarperCollins books may be purchased for educational, business, or sales promotional use. For information, please email the Special Markets Department at SPsales@harpercollins.com.

FIRST EDITION

Designed by Yvonne Chan
Illustrations by Yvonne Chan / © HarperCollins Publishers

Library of Congress Cataloging-in-Publication Data has been applied for.

ISBN 978-0-06-290637-3
ISBN 978-0-06-298270-4 (B&N)
ISBN 978-0-06-298509-5 (signed)

19 20 21 22 23   LSC   10 9 8 7 6 5 4 3 2

Disclaimer: Some names and identifying details have been changed to protect the privacy of individuals. In these instances, original names have been replaced with Russian aliases because I'm obsessed with the Romanovs, thanks to the animated classic *Anastasia*. And don't even get me started on Russian gymnastics.

Sensitivity warning: While this book has hilarious fun moments, it also discusses tough issues. While there aren't graphic details, if you're a survivor of sexual abuse, or struggling with addiction, please utilize the resources pages in the back of this book.

Imperfection is beautiful.

To anyone who has ever felt broken

beyond repair, this is for you.

If you've ever been excluded,

or told you were not enough,

know that you are enough,

and beautifully complete.

CONTENTS

OVER THE TOP

CHAPTER 1

ALL THE PARTS

YOU KNOW THOSE PLANTS THAT ARE ALWAYS TRYING TO FIND THE light? Maybe they were planted in a location that didn't necessarily facilitate growth, but inexplicably they make a circuitous route to not only survive but bloom into a beautiful plant. That was me—my whole life. But extremely flamboyantly jubilant and oh so gay. Picture me in the seventh grade: a chubby, slightly snaggletoothed kid with a voluminous mop of frizzy curly hair that screamed through layers of gel for what I desperately wanted to be a Hanson-esque, smooth collarbone-length center-parted man-bob. I'd be cycling through several of my cutest looks, usually monochromatic jumpers with severe Doc Martens boots, just to go to the mall. It felt entirely possible that a talent scout would be there, in the nation's smallest capital of Springfield, Illinois, on the off-weekend my family was there for a soccer tournament with my brothers, just waiting outside Claire's to discover a kid like me and guide me to center stage. I'd practice ice-skating routines in my living room, trying to be like the Olympians I idolized, imagining how triumphant I'd be when I finally seized that gold medal. With a cute enough outfit and the right attitude (yet no ability to skate, flip, or sing), I could become a Michelle Kwan–, Dominique Dawes–, or Christina Aguilera–level hero. And maybe, just maybe, someday I'd get out of Quincy, Illinois. (And by "someday," I meant: as soon as physically possible.)

The years of fantasizing about reaching stratospheric fame through a local mall discovery had long since faded by 2017. I'd settled for much more attainable goals. I became a hairdresser, working in both LA and New York. I'd stumbled, very gratefully, into a side hustle in the form of a web series called *Gay of Thrones*. That spring I would move to Atlanta to shoot a dream project with four new friends. We had beaten out the collective gay world for these five coveted positions, and we all knew it was a monumental opportunity. Like Maya Angelou taught me, I was hoping for the best, but preparing for the worst, so that nothing could catch me off guard. I was just happy that I had completed my mission of escaping cornfield-small-town-only-gay-person infamy and was now free to live an authentic queer life in a gorgeous big city with a Trader Joe's and nobody thinking twice about my leggings.

A year later in February, *Queer Eye* had just come out, and I was on my way to a meeting at *Town & Country*. Do I know what you do at magazine meetings? Absolutely not! But I've seen enough *America's Next Top Model* seasons to know how to nail a go-see.

To my shock I arrived early, so I went to grab a coffee, and as I was walking in, this lady with the most gorgeous expertly done microbraids and giant glasses stopped me and bellowed, "Honey, this faggotry you are serving is giving me everything!"

At first, I was confused. Did she just call me a fag? But the smile on her face and her extreme proximity seemed to suggest a loving and enamored person. I'm now doubly confused, I'm running ahead of schedule, and strangers are stopping me. Mind you, it's still 8:15 a.m., my eyes still subtly perma-stoned from last night's edible, and I hadn't even had my coffee yet! So I said, "Thanks, queen," and continued on my way.

But then two steps later, two other girls stopped me. They said they were living for the show and asked if they could take selfies. Of course I said, "Yes, sweets!" and that caused a few more girls from outside the shop to come in for what was quickly becoming an impromptu meet-and-greet. My original encounter from the store got in line for her pic next, then became the photographer for the rest of the meet-and-greet. After thanking all my new friends, I left the coffee shop to head back to *Town & Country* with no coffee because I forgot. *Well, that was fun. How much am I thriving right now?* I thought.

Crossing the street to go to my meeting, a very nice man stopped me and began playing twenty questions with me about my life, about the show, about everything. I obliged, because I'm eternally a people pleaser, and I didn't want him to feel bad, but at that point my early arrival turned into being fully actually late to the meeting. I tried to explain that to him as I was frolicking away like a gorgeous gazelle toward the doors of the Hearst building.

When I was filming *Queer Eye* in secrecy with the boys in Atlanta in 2017, sometimes producers, or people who were familiar with the show's revival, would ask me, "Are you ready for your life to change?" I always said, "OMG, yes! So excited to not keep a secret, and I've definitely been stopped by fans for, like, three to seven selfies a day once a year when I go to Pride, so I'm totally ready!" How different would my day-to-day life really be? I'd been going about my life, just business as usual, the same way it had always been. But this morning, something shifted. People knew who I was, everywhere I went.

There was a girl who stopped me on the corner of Twenty-Third and Park not long after the show came out. We made eye contact for a split second and it was like an invisible Jackie Chan punched her in the stomach. She doubled over. She took a dramatic step back. "Oh my God," she yelled. "Oh my God! Oh my God!" I was so worried about her that I stopped right there and pulled her onto the curb. We sat for a while until she pulled herself together.

It surprised me how often people would stop me, becoming deeply vulnerable about the way the show had changed their lives. Most of the time it would hit me in a really gorgeous place. But other times it would be painfully triggering to hear about their pain and what they were struggling with. Sometimes I was tempted to give people my phone number, and at times would until my mom impressed upon me how unwise this was. In therapy I had learned about "selective permeability" (a term that pertains to cellular membranes letting some, but not all, molecules enter the cell; the same can apply to interacting with people—not taking on the experiences or negativity of others, but staying open to accepting joy or gratitude) but although I had practiced that behind the chair at work as a hair stylist, I had never had to exercise those muscles so nimbly anywhere anytime with strangers so often. Learning to hold a safe space for people to share with me while maintaining my well-being is a delicate dance.

When people had asked me whether I was ready for my life to change, I don't think I really understood what they meant. It wasn't just that strangers would know who I was. It was this other thing that started to happen to me: when I looked in their eyes, sometimes, there was a little voice in my head wondering,

Would you still be so excited to meet me if you really knew who I was? If you knew all the things I'd done? If you could see all my parts?

Sure, there's a part of me that's endlessly positive. But it's just one part. It's a beautiful part, a strong part, and an important part, but it's not all of it. There are other parts I want to show, parts that are a little bit scarier to get into. Like the nagging, insecure part of me that worries my positivity is faker than the hair that covers the chalkboard scalp of Donald Trump. Or the part of me that's had sex with a ton of people—a lot of whom I wish I hadn't. What about my irritated part, which isn't the easiest to deal with if my people-pleasing part has been working overtime. My binge-eating part, my part that just wants to be left alone, or my part that could make you pray for me to catch permanent laryngitis because I can't stop telling you about the Romanovs, or my cats, or the irony of the GOP that wants low taxes and even lower federal government regulation, *unless* it comes to regulation of people's pregnancies, marijuana, or the fundamentally racist state and federal prison systems. Because when you have this much personality, there's a fear lurking just below the surface: If you knew all of me, you wouldn't love me anymore. You would no longer want me as your new best friend.

I love an uplifting, feel-good moment. I love everything packaged up neatly and put into an easily understandable box. I continue to realize that this is not how life works. Joy can live beside sorrow. Life is messy, unpredictable, and seldom tied into neat little boxes. This book is a moment for me to share with you what I have learned so far. There's a rhyme and reason behind my effervescent spirit, and no, I did not wake up like this. It took a lot of trauma and tears to become the person you see today. Sometimes I think people only want to see the side of me that's power stomping in stilettos, or spinning around on figure skates. But this book is my chance to show you more. It's not gonna be pretty, but it's my truth, and if I don't share it, I won't be able to help others who are struggs to func.

Brené Brown is an incredible researcher, author, and speaker who has taught me 60 percent of what I know about vulnerability, courage, and authenticity. I look up to her work and her teachings so much. She talks about what shame is, and who to be vulnerable with, which has gone into my thinking for this venture a lot. She says shame is the feeling of, "If you knew all there was to know about me, you wouldn't love me anymore," which always struck a chord with me. Also to be vulnerable with people who earn it, and I thought about that in writing this book too. I want a world with more feel-good queer stories. Being LGBTQ+ doesn't mean a life of certain pain and suffering—actually, yes it does because that's what life is for everyone—but I want more queer stories that are light and not full of pain and abuse. But that's not really possible. Joy and pain often occur all together. No matter our orientation, to live is to experience suffering at some point. Historically, we have had more heteronormative stories being told; our LGBTQ+ family members just now in the past few decades are getting a seat at the storytelling table.

Shame loves secrets, it thrives with them. I'm telling my story to help myself heal, and remove the shame, in the hope that this might help others heal too. I feel at this time in my life, with all the work I've done on myself, that I'm strong enough to be this vulnerable. After experiencing such an outpouring of love, I believe anyone reading this has earned my honesty.

* * *

Like any consumer of pop culture, I've watched celebrity breakdowns, read salacious stories, and asked myself, "Who does that?"–never realizing that I could be in a position to be under the same kind of scrutiny. I grew up in a small town where my family's business, as part owners of a broadcast media company, made us well known in a way that was, for me, suffocating. We were basically a not-as-popular, local version of the Kennedys, and I was, obviously, incredibly gay. I used to live for this vision of moving to a big city where nobody knew who I was, and I could just walk down the street, completely anonymous. That was always the dream. So what did I think was going to happen if I went on a TV show? Hollywood is just its own small town, after all.

It never occurred to me that if I ever really found success in the entertainment industry, I would be sacrificing the anonymity I'd wanted so badly. It was like my very own Gift of the Magi. Back when I was hoping for the best but preparing for the worst, I never really thought about what "the best" would actually entail.

It wasn't as if I didn't already have some familiarity with what celebrity was like. My first week working as an assistant at a famous hair salon in LA, I washed a well-known actress's hair. Soon I was assisting hairdressers working with major celebrity clients. I could name-drop, but ew, queen. Let's just say, I encountered celebrities aplenty. I saw how fame seemed to change different people: Some of them treat you like you're to be seen and not heard. Some of them treat you like you're talent too. When I became a main hairstylist, I would see how a few of them were mean to my assistant, even if they were nice to me. It showed me that celebrities are all very human. They have their own fears and their own darkness, too, no matter what you think you know.

But living in a world where it's so easy to take everyone's highly curated Instagram feed at face value, it's important to dig deeper, to read between the lines, to see through all of it and not compare yourself to them! Comparing ourselves to people on social media is as risky as using WebMD to diagnose yourself. You'll end up way more stressed than before—just don't even go there. Comparison is that stop we can just ride on past because it smells bad and is relentlessly draining.

People mostly know me for being positive and loving. But part of being fearlessly, endlessly encouraging is also giving voice to the parts you don't want seen—like the part that snaps when it gets riled. I wouldn't want most people seeing that irritated part—the part of me that comes out if my assistant leaves my client's toner on for too long and fucks up her color. You don't want to be with me in the back room when I'm telling her, "I'm elbow-deep in highlights trying to fix the same mistake you've made twice this week." You can't be fiercely loving without also being passionate—and sometimes passionate isn't pretty. What might seem testy is actually scar tissue, the residual effects of trauma that I lived through.

So that's the question that I keep coming back to. Would you love me if you saw me in a bad moment? Would you love me if I'm momentarily Grumps McGee about everybody taking forever? Would you love me if you saw all my parts?

The whole parts thing is really ferosh, but I didn't come up with it. It actually came from this doctor, Richard C. Schwartz, who created something called internal family systems therapy. According to him, we were all born as a centered self, who is perfect and whole and can handle anything. But as we experience trauma in life, the centered self doesn't know quite how to deal with it, so it develops pieces of ourselves that we can call upon based on the situations we find ourselves in. It's not as intense as multiple personality disorder—it's more, like, we all have these parts in our personality, but some people's are more extreme or polarized than others.

The work you do in this modality of therapy is about getting the parts to talk to one another. If you think of your personality like a car, it's like this: My busy bee sits in the driver's seat, saying yes to every job coming my way with no thought for overbooking. Kicking out my people pleaser who's now in the passenger seat, and then my inner child is in the car seat. Meanwhile, my inner critic, who has the voice of grandmother, can't stop backseat driving and telling everyone how I could be driving so much more effectively, and since we're in a minivan, my narrator in the back seat can't stop talking about the geopolitical climate of Venezuela but simultaneously also wants to talk about this year's World Gymnastics Championships. What's that noise coming from the top of the car? Oh, I think that's my raunchy sex kitten in a tube dress, doing Lizzo ass-clap-twerk-practice to post up to her Insta story. That's right: My personality is a minivan, actually a small bus. There are different pieces of me that are all driving together, with one in charge based on what's happening in my life. Ideally, you get the parts to realize that they're all in the same car—and they're all trying to help, but your centered self is actually capable of driving you back to a safe, soothing place.

This is a book about all my parts, and how I learned to integrate them: the part of me that's funny and the part of me that's still wounded and fragile and the part of me that's loving and the part of me that's kind of a diva and the part of me that's read the Bhagavad Gita and the Bible and *The Four Agreements* and is still Postmatesing twelve-dollar coffees and screaming about my first-world problems. And it's a book too about the part of me that I'm really scared to talk about: the part that's been psychotically depressed and self-destructive, to the point where I truly did not care what happened to me.

It's scary for me to share my truth. But I've had a lot of practice getting comfortable with what that truth is. And I'm ready to let you in too. So I'm telling my story—the whole story—to show that some masterpieces start off a mess. Sort of like the girl who stopped me on the street that day in New York, the one who totally lost her shit. After she pulled herself together, we did a full-fledged photo shoot, right there on the corner of Twenty-Third and Park. Did it begin as a near bus crash? Certainly. But it ended as a glamorous content session, crisis averted, content created, both of our days made.

CHAPTER 2

JACK

BEFORE THERE WAS JVN, THERE WAS JACK. THAT'S WHAT EVERYONE called me when I was a kid. I didn't start going by Jonathan until I started hair school at age eighteen. Baby Jack had his passions, and they rotated with the seasons.

First, there was winter. My brother and his bounding straight-boy energy, which was like nails on a chalkboard to my gay self, would be at soccer or baseball tournaments. I would be in the living room, watching the figure skaters in the Olympics. (Or, if it was a non-Olympic year, it would be one of the six events of the ISU Grand Prix competition leading up to nationals, then worlds, or maybe a pro tournament with Katarina Witt and Kristi Yamaguchi.) I was not a casual watcher of figure skating–any Olympic sport that was on TV on a Saturday or Sunday would dominate my world. Tennis. Volleyball.

Track and field. Synchronized swimming. Diving. Moguls. Aerials. Long jumping. Speed skating. *Honey*. Any major network sports special that wasn't heteronormative—I was here for it.

But I was here for nothing more than the two sports that really blew my gay brain and made me into the adult that I am today: figure skating and gymnastics. Of these two sports, I watched every moment available to me. Like my life depended on it. All of them. Nancy Kerrigan, who lost her gold with no fall, which was controversial, but those judges had had it with the Harding and Kerrigan American figure-skating scandal, so Oksana Baiul won out in '94. And don't even get me started on the fact that 1992 was the last year they had winter and summer games in the same year, and then in 1992 the International Olympic Committee decided it would be cuter if they alternated them in two-year cycles, which is why Michelle Kwan, the love of my life, is an Olympic silver medalist and bronze medalist instead of a two-time Olympic gold medalist, because she was untouchable in 1996 and 2000. No one could even think about touching her. But talk about accepting what is with grace and dignity and being the queen you are, Michelle Kwan.

Anyway, I'd watch the Olympics and make two cinnamon and brown sugar Pop-Tarts in the toaster, eat two more of them cold while the other two were toasting, then wash that down with a few powdered donuts. After the figure skating was over, I'd go on the trampoline and if it wasn't too snowy I'd do my own gymnastics routines, pretending that I was winning world championships—and if I messed up, it was always okay, because that was really just the short program, and I still had the long to create an epic comeback story, which also meant that we had some beautiful interstitial vignettes to film before we went back inside to finish the last of the family-size pack of cinnamon brown sugar Pop-Tarts (or maybe s'mores—those were great too) and the last few Diet Pepsis from the cube. (That's two twelve-packs on top of each other to make a twenty-four-pack.)

The 1992 Olympics were in Barcelona, but I felt like I was right there with them. It was the first time the US women's gymnastics team had ever won a medal—we took bronze—and I was so proud of my girls. I loved their g-force-proof hair spray fringes and how athletic they were. I wanted to be their best friends, to do flips with them, to be a fierce gymnast just like them. I would stand up and wave to the walls and pretend like I just stuck my landing, imitating their grace and their poise. If Shannon Miller could fill the void that Kim Zmeskal left in the women's individual all-around and come through as the American hero that she was with that silver medal (which should have been gold, even though that gold medalist was fierce too; Shan-Shan got screwed, much like Beyoncé got screwed to Adele in the 2017 Grammys)—if Shannon could do that, then I too could be graceful on my little midwestern cornfield.

Maybe most of all, I loved the little montages where you saw where they came from, their origin stories. A little song would play over footage of the gymnast with her family in her hometown, and she'd say something like, "My mom and I drive three hours to and back from the gym every day, and even though people overlook and underestimate me, I know if I work hard I can make it." (Which is literally Shannon Miller's story, because all the world was focused on Kim Zmeskal since she was the first American woman to win the individual all-around at the World Gymnastics Championships, in 1991, so everyone thought she was going to come in '92 and be the next Mary Lou Retton, but—pressure!—Shannon Miller stepped in and came out with silver in the individual all-around, even though she was an under-the-radar baby diva with a paper-towel-roll fringe to boot.)

Those little vignettes gave my life purpose. So did Michelle Kwan. So did Kim Zmeskal. So did Shannon Miller. These stories were my motivation toward ferocity.

And compared to the truly titillating content on MTV at the time, figure skating was just good wholesome fun. Don't get me wrong, I loved sneaking a peek at the softcore that was early '90s music videos, but that took major effort, even when my parents weren't around and I was left with my babysitter, Natalya. She had an unfortunately boxy perm and very high-waisted pants (usually salmon-colored, but sometimes seafoam green) and a terrible attitude. She made a hamburger casserole, though, that was so good it would make your dead grandma cry. Natalya was always getting in the way when I was trying to watch Madonna videos. "You can't watch this!" she'd snap, turning it off. It made me feel so ashamed—I just wanted to hump a pillow to "Erotica" in peace! I wanted to chill to a Madonna music video marathon and let her hot backup dancers soothe me. Life was hard enough without Natalya's heteronormativity.

But the Olympics—those everyone could agree on. I watched them with my family, because we were the kind of family who thought that was cool. Which I think is great! More families should watch the Olympics together. To me, those are core American family values: Cheering on a corrupt institutional body that's super problematic with money and opportunity but we all pretend like it's an equal playing field and celebrate it—what's more American than that?

I tried to do gymnastics, or what we would now call power tumbling, because they took it one step further to make it less "gay" to the boys, so at the end of the tumble track would be a basketball hoop where other boys would do flips and dunk, making it less threatening to their straightness. All the other boys were actually really good at tumbling, but I wasn't. I had no core strength, so I just used my momentum to hurtle my big gay body through space. Also, I couldn't go backward because I was deathly afraid. But I never gave up.

Another thing I learned from these vignettes was that there was always an extremely involved parent putting all their hopes and dreams and failures into the sparkly leotard promises of their child's talent and nonstop training. My mom was an account executive in the advertising section at the local newspaper. She didn't have time to ride my back all the way to the Olympics. I would have gotten myself there with my work ethic and passion and drive—I was sure of it. I could have been Adam Rippon if somebody had only made the time. If I could go back in time, I'd yell at my mom to stop her newspaper advertising excellence, find a damn ice-skating rink, and cheerfully drive me the two hours to Springfield, Illinois, or the two and a half hours to St. Louis five mornings a week like a normal parent. Am I asking for so much here? I could have been an expressive-arm-movements-on-the-ice prodigy, or at the very least an ice dancer. Instead, I had to wait until I was a grown woman to get an apartment in New York City two blocks away from an ice-skating rink so I could live in relentless pursuit of my Olympic truth. (But also, Mom, thanks so much for giving me clothes and feeding me and raising me, I love you so much! Also, how much fun was that when we watched *Bewitched* and *The Mary Tyler Moore Show* together? Nick at Nite used to be really good.)

I tried Boy Scouts, and that didn't go much better. I finally convinced my mom to let me quit after a hideous experience at paper airplane assembly. All the boys lined up and one at a time had to throw their airplanes across an emptied-out cafeteria. With one limp wrist, at exactly ninety degrees to the ground, a pointed toe, and all the good intentions in the world, I released my paper airplane—only for it to land behind me. All the other Boy Scouts laughed. "Give it another two weeks!" my mom said, but I was done. I didn't have anything to talk to them about! It didn't help that I was extremely knowledgeable about the Miss America and Miss Universe organizations and was ready, willing, and able to talk ad nauseam about it to anyone who entered a three-cubic-foot radius of me. Whether you were a six-year-old boy or a seventy-year-old woman, I was ready to gab. Is that so wrong?

So I'd stay home, watching my girls. I'd embrace a gorgeous Tower of Pizza moment (my favorite hometown restaurant ever, the second of which would be El Rancherito—pepperoni, sausage, and onion pizza, with so much white cheese dip) and watch a great episode of *Dateline* with Stone Phillips and Jane Pauley, or some episodes of *The Nanny*, and every so often there would be a Bowflex commercial and I'd gaze, mesmerized, at the shape of the man's chest in the ad. I wanted to run him down. *Why am I so soft?* I wondered. *Why doesn't my body look like that? When am I gonna get my abdominals? Why don't I get to nuzzle my face into some gorgeous pecs?* And then I'd put the thought away for a while and eat some more. That was a perfect winter day.

Then there was the perfect spring day, which would happen at my grandparents' condo in Florida, where my mom would whisk me away for our birthdays, which fall a day apart, and I would play hooky from school for a couple days. In the mornings my grandma would make me the most voluptuous breakfast: Cinnamon Toast Crunch with a cup of Café Français, this delicious instant coffee she had, and two cinnamon rolls from a tin container of four, with ooey-gooey realness in the middle, and I'd eat the beginning of the roll and when I got to the center I'd scrape this ball of cinnamon sugar out with my fork—truly, it was everything. Except for when I needed a third, and my grandma would fat-shame me by saying two was enough, and I'd say, "Anne! I need a third cinnamon roll!" I went through them quickly. We'd have to go to the grocery store to hunt them down, and they became harder and harder to find. After this one year, they had just fully disappeared from the grocery store, and we had to switch to Pillsbury, which really wasn't the same. If anyone at Sara Lee is reading this and knows how I can get those back, please hit a bitch up. Let's get some research and development going and bring back a classic. Reboots are in these days.

In addition to the Cinnamon Toast Crunch and instant coffee and cinnamon rolls, there were four pieces of bacon and a little cup of orange juice, and eventually my grandpa would lumber out in his bathrobe and eat eight full pieces of whole wheat toast with I Can't Believe It's Not Butter while we watched *The Today Show*.

Those spring days were perfect, too, because they gave me six whole days out of Quincy, a desperately needed respite from the constant feeling of not fitting in and being bullied and always having to fight to have a little safety. I didn't have the vocabulary then to explain just how much every day was a battle. Being removed from that battle and plopped next to a gorgeous tranquil beach with your witty grandmother who took no shit and loved to chat was really essential to baby Jack's sanity—and while I loved my brothers, it gave me six whole days with my mom where I didn't have to compete for her attention from the rest of my family or her demanding work duties. My mom was my moon, my sun, and my stars. It meant so much to me to be away from everything with her. When I started to realize it was coming to an end, I felt a bottomless pit grow wider within me that only buying a gaggle of guinea pigs would eventually fill. (But it took at least six years of convincing my mom to even get those guinea pigs—it didn't happen until 1999. The last one, Teddy, died the same day Ronald Reagan died in 2004. His brothers and sisters were named Sugar, Emma, and Nut-Nut. His parents were named Nilly and Nut the First.)

It all made me want to control what I could, which brings me to fall, when I would make little stations for myself that took me through my day: an hour sitting at the kitchen table watching

TV and eating dry Cap'n Crunch, then an hour playing tennis with myself against the garage door, then an hour watching TV on the couch while I ate more dry Cap'n Crunch, then an hour choreographing some gorgeous carpet figure skating, then an hour calling the six people on my phone list to walk around and chat for an hour, then an hour practicing the violin, which always made my dog Ginny groan from a guttural place in her belly, then laboriously get up and wander outside to get away from the noise. And every year we would make hot apple cider—real apple cider from the apple orchards outside Quincy, and I'd get to play with the kittens and eat honeycomb and eventually I probably would throw a temper tantrum because I wanted to go rollerblading instead.

But the most perfect, absolutely flaw-free kind of day could only happen in the summertime. And it was in the summer that I figured out, for the first time, exactly who I wanted to be.

In Quincy, Illinois, if you were of a certain group of upper-middle-class people, your children would spend their summers at Quincy Country Club. And let me tell you, it was gorgeous.

First of all, there were the pool ladies. In every country club watering hole across America there's a group of glamorous pool moms. Early on Saturday mornings, all the most fabulous matriarchs would parade out of the changing room, nab the best recliner chairs, layer on the tanning oil, and gossip their faces off. While the rest of the little boys were peeing in the water, shooting their Nerf water guns, or playing some capture the flag game, you could find me gossiping with a group of the most notorious pool ladies. We would talk manis and pedis, whether so-and-so had ever tried a certain face mask, or if they had heard that another lady had left her husband for her female secretary. They helped foster my love of beauty by reading magazines with me and talking shit about everyone else's hair.

I loved a pool chair moment, but the real action took place over by the cabanas. That's where they served the jumbo pretzels, chicken fingers, nacho cheese, and ranch dressing and marinara sauce and ketchup with some mayonnaise on it—that's a quadruple-threat dipping sauce situation, but who's counting?—and ice cream sandwiches. But more importantly, that's where the cabana girls hung out.

That's where so many of my formative memories come from—in the shaded part of a cabana where I would concession-stand like there was no tomorrow. The cabana was attended to by these teenage models with names like Stacey and Nicole. (I also wished that I had been named Stacey or Nicole, but it wasn't in the cards.) They wore uniforms that included these little white pillbox hats, and underneath them, they wore their hair in these cute little low-slung buns and permed ponytail configurations. This was, like, 1991, so all the boys had this long, shaggy hair tucked behind their ears. So messy and gross. And here these fabulous girls were, parading around with style. I was obsessed with that silhouette, with that little chic hat and low-slung bun. I was all about it. They were young and beautiful and they owned that pool deck. I wanted to grow out my hair, walk fiercely with trays, and be the cabana girl boss of my dreams.

One day during a gossip sesh, I asked the pool ladies what you call the people who do hair and they told me that if you wanted to do it all—the hair, the makeup, the nails, and even give massages—you had to be a cosmetologist.

So later that summer when my dad's incredibly gorgeous, super-masc best friend asked me what I wanted to be when I grew up, I said without any hesitation at all, "I want to be a cabana girl—or a cosmetologist." I can still see the shocked look on his handsome, stubbly face as he asked me what a four-year-old could possibly know about cosmetology. I calmly replied that it was someone who perms hair, does nails, or even gives massages, because cosmetologists get to do it all—just like one of the fabulous pool ladies had told me.

He blinked slowly, three times. In that moment, he'd helped me realize my dreams. That was the first time I remember seriously considering becoming a hairdresser.

It fit for me: I didn't know it then, but to anyone's untrained eye, I was clearly extremely gay. And soon enough, I'd see for myself that growing up feminine in a rural midwestern town was . . . difficult. In a gorgeous way. When I say "gorgeous," that's really a coping mechanism for me to make light of the fact that it wasn't gorgeous. That same man told me weeks later that I couldn't sit back in the cabana and help anymore. We couldn't have a little boy wearing the girls' pillbox hats and pretending to be a waitress, could we?

But I've always been in touch with my feminine side. I loved to carry purses with checkbooks, pens, ChapStick, and little baby things for my Cabbage Patch doll. I wanted to be a modern mom on the go just like my mom. I wanted to wear dresses, rock heals, play with makeup. But I could also be into the WWF wrestling my brothers were obsessed with. I could wear boy clothes. I could be boyish when necessary, but identifying male and female in the same day is something that has always been possible for me. The binary always has felt like something that I didn't quite fit in to. As a kid this presented itself in a lot ways. I had two cousins, Anastasia and Stanislava—obviously those aren't their real names, but remember we are concealing people's identities using glamorous Russian pseudonyms—and when we were little, we would play with evening gowns. I loved everything about beauty pageants. I guess I have always felt gender queer, either both of the genders or somewhere in the middle. I just never knew that had a name that I could identify with. I was really quick to put on heels and a gorgeous puffy-shouldered evening gown. That really terrified my father. I remember him walking in and me being torn out of this poufy black gown, and then there was a new rule that I wasn't allowed to play dress-up with my cousins. But my aunt Ludmila wasn't really about that, so we'd sneakily play with whatever we wanted, though it sometimes took an hour and a half to get out of it and hide the glitter before I went back home to my dad's house.

Here's what I imagine was going through my dad's brain: *A boy playing with makeup? Impossible. A boy wants to carry a purse? Not my son! Find a boy playing dress-up in an evening gown? Tear it off his body. A boy playing with Barbies? Panic. This cannot be my son's life. I will shake, scare, and rattle it out of him. This has to be a phase.* I knew my dad loved me, but he was a young father doing his best to come to terms with what was, for him, a scary reality.

I didn't need gigantic *Divine Secrets of the Ya-Ya Sisterhood* moments to know that there was something wrong with me. I got plenty of cues from other kids, from my parents, from my grandparents. When I danced: "Do your movements have to be so flimsy?" my grandma asked. When I developed a devout binding obsession with Hanson and all I wanted was to grow out my hair, but lacked the patience and tenacity it took to get there, so I would put the back of my hair into a mini-ponytail with my fringe out, the boys at school would point at me—sort of a mean and straight version of Karen from *Will and Grace* saying, "What's this, what's that, what's going on here?"

The thing is, I had a lot of secrets already, even as a little kid. There was a multitude of reasons my personality was bigger than Dolly Parton's hair. There was an emptiness I was trying to fill, an unspeakable shame I was trying to soothe. So many things I wasn't able to talk about yet. Why was I so nervous around my dad's immaculately handsome, hairy-chested best friend? Why did being in the YMCA locker room send my heart aflutter? Why was it that the other boys wanted to ride bikes and I wanted to figure out how to blow-dry my Barbie's hair without melting her face? Why did I have flashbacks at night of events that didn't feel right but no matter what, I couldn't give voice to? There was nobody to tell about that kind of shame and pain. So creating pockets of joy for myself was an art I learned early.

* * *

Maybe it was only because I was so lonely that I was able to make a space in my imagination to be so free. At some point I started choreographing my own carpet figure-skating routines. Even if I had no one to share my deepest secrets with, I could still dance on my own, anyway, and find a space I was passionate about. Those moments of freedom gave me all the little endorphin hits I needed to connect the dark trenches of loneliness together and find a little light.

From figure-skating routines, I progressed to balance beam routines and trampoline stick-it competitions. By the time I was ten I had won enough imaginary gold medals for the USA to be Shannon Miller, Simone Biles, and Aly Raisman.

It was a lesson for me. Even in my loneliest times, I knew I could go deep into my imagination and create a better reality for myself, and that spilled into my life in so many other areas. Those little moments kept me expanding instead of shrinking into myself. If my passion for life was a flame, so many people were trying to figure out how to douse water on it—but I kept it burning within myself. No amount of homophobic, misogynistic fuckery was going to pull me out of that.

People love to say "Be yourself"—but for me, there was no choice! I was too gorgeously myself, with femininity dripping from every pore—I had no option to be anything but myself. She's as gay as they come, honey. I can't even do a straight accent—it's not in my repertoire.

I lived for an opportunity to make my world more fun and beautiful. And every so often, I'd have an opportunity to bring that vivacious flair to more than just my Olympic performances. In kindergarten, my teacher, Mrs. Tashlikova, announced that we would be doing a pumpkin decorating contest. When my mom picked me up from school, I screamed, "Mom, Mom, Mom! We're doing a pumpkin decorating contest!"

"Oh, Jackie, that'll be so fun!" she said. "Let's go to the store and get our supplies together. I think it would be really cute to make a mouth out of two tortilla chips and get a kidney bean to use for a tongue." Now you see where I get my imagination.

I *knew* that this was the cutest most award-winning idea of literally all time. My mom worked a lot—from eight in the morning until eight o'clock at night—so she wasn't always around to help me with school projects. But this day was special. We had a vision. I was sure we would win. My mom? Please. Her creativity was unparalleled. At the very least I was certain we'd make the top three.

We set all the materials up on the kitchen counter. We carved a pumpkin that had the cutest green apple eyes with red pepper lips. "Or," my mom said, "we could do a green eyebrow."

"Let's create a banana nose!" I said.

By the time we were done, we had served a pumpkin face that was truly orig.

The next day was the judging part of the competition. In the hallway, we all put our pumpkins up on a display case, so on the way into class, everyone had a chance to look at all the pumpkins, then vote. After recess, the winners were announced. These flawed-ass, small-town, no-creativity-having kids had the nerve to not even vote my pumpkin in the top five. I hadn't been this rattled by an unexpected result since Ross Perot's unprecedented third-party candidacy took over 19 million votes, which was 18.91 percent of the popular vote in the 1992 presidential election.

I was rattled to my core. I was sure we'd been unceremoniously robbed. Were people jealous of our family because of the newspaper? It was my first introduction to the cruel reality that haters can be jealous. And Haterade does not taste better cold, or room temperature. It's very bitter, and hurtful.

This part of me—this little wounded chubby feminine kid inside—was an easy target.

* * *

What would have already been a tough childhood, considering my limp wrist and penchant for sequins, was made tougher by some very early, very confusing encounters that would end up coloring the rest of my life.

In the church I grew up going to, I went to Sunday school with a group of kids. Sometimes Sunday school was held at a church family's house, and afterward we would all gather to socialize. There was an older boy who taught me to play a game called Doctor. I would usually end up in a closet missing some of my clothes and not quite sure of exactly what happened—but I felt a heartbeat that I wasn't used to feeling in my chest, and a nauseating excitement inside that left me feeling a shame that I'd never experienced before.

At the dinner table, we always talked about what we learned at school that day. One night my mom asked my brother Timofei what he'd studied in school.

"We learned about HIV!" Timofei said.

"What did you learn about it?" my mom asked.

"We learned that you get it when two boys have sex."

I dropped my fork. I could feel the color drain out of my face. Tears were streaming down my cheeks before I even knew why. I jumped off my chair and bolted out of the room.

I sat on the bottom of the stairs, sobbing. My mom came after me. "What's wrong?" she asked. "Jackie, what's wrong?"

I told her what had happened with the boy from church. I saw her face twist up in an expression I didn't recognize. "Where did he touch you?" she said. "What exactly happened?"

I couldn't really get the words out. I felt so ashamed, even before I had the language to know what shame was.

The next afternoon, we met in the living room to have a "family meeting"—to talk about what had happened to me. I know that my mom was trying to get ahead of the issue and resolve it, and to undo any damage done to me, but sexual abuse—having your little-kid world painted in colors that you don't understand—can't be painted into a neat little box right away. It's not something for which you can shake the Etch-a-Sketch and have it not be so. Once it's happened, you can't change it back.

I was so embarrassed that my dad knew what had happened to me, that my brothers knew about it too. I wasn't exactly sure what I was saying or how it was going to impact anyone.

"Experimentation is normal," my mom said patiently. "But we'll never go over there again."

I nodded.

From the rest of my family there was a definite sense that I was just doing it for the attention, which was almost more damaging than it happening in the first place. But I know that this happens a lot: Nobody wants to believe that their family member or sibling or child has been molested. It's so much easier for people to think they're fabricating, embellishing, or confused—or that they're a co-conspirator in it—than it is to really sit with the reality of what happened.

Which was that an older boy took advantage of a four-year-old, which was not okay, no matter how you slice that particular pie.

I love a box. I love no loose ends. I love a clearly processed idea. Taco Bell is my favorite fast food because she's as processed as it gets. But in this case, my introduction to my sexuality needed to be processed, not tucked away in a neat little box never to be seen or heard from again.

But that's exactly what we did.

* * *

That same year, one night after dinner, I was watching *Looney Tunes*. It might have been *Road Runner*. (I also lived for Tom and Jerry, and the NRA-card-carrying Elmer Fudd.)

"Boys, come into the bedroom!" I heard my mom call. I followed my brothers into my parents' bedroom and sat down on the floor, crisscross applesauce, on the emerald-green carpet, sandwiched between the water bed and a white wicker loveseat—all of which created a bedroom so painfully '80s it could have been ripped from a period sitcom.

"Boris, Timofei, Jack," my dad said. He cleared his throat. "Your mom and I love you very much and we want you to know that we will always love you. That will never change." Timofei put his head in his hands and I felt the room shift. Kind of like in *Twister*, when Bill Paxton picks up that handful of dirt and lets it ominously sift through his fingers, like, *Oh no, there's about to be an F3*. Something was going down.

"Your dad and I are going to get a divorce," my mom said. "But that doesn't mean anyone did something wrong." (Even in that moment, she was diplomatic AF.) "This is nobody's fault."

"Nuh-uh," Boris said, and then he began to sob, and then Timofei was sobbing too. A silence filled the room. Everyone was crying except for me. Only one thing came to my mind.

"Can I have the ring?" I said.

"What ring?" my mom asked.

"Your wedding ring," I said. I loved the diamond, but what really caught my eye were the sapphire stones on the outside of the main diamond, which I knew was something that would exponentially increase the value of my geode collection. As an avid rock collector, I knew how to spot a good find when I saw one.

Everyone laughed. "No," she said. "You can't have the ring."

I didn't understand how this was going to impact my life—how could I? Divorce was just something I'd heard Matt Lauer and Katie Couric talk about when they discussed how high the divorce rate was (along with the five-hundred-year flood, which was happening that year, in 1993). All I really knew was that I'd be one of those kids now.

The day after they told us, my brothers and I dressed our obese yellow lab, Ginny, in Umbro shorts, a basketball jersey, and sunglasses and took her to their bedroom, where they were still sleeping together in bed, to wake them up. We thought maybe they'd see how cute the dog was and how funny we could be and decide to take it back, to not get divorced after all.

It didn't work.

I didn't cry about it, maybe because I still didn't totally understand what was happening. Plus, I wasn't enthralled by my dad's company, anyway. He wasn't around much, and his temper was fierce. He had an exceptionally low tolerance for spills, messes, and feminine behavior, which—as you can imagine—didn't bode well for baby me. So I wasn't upset that he'd be moving out—but everyone else was so upset, so I tried to act like I was too.

Mostly I hid away with my gorgeous highly processed kid snacks and my figure skaters on TV. Those girls gave me a glimpse into grace and female badassery I hadn't yet experienced in my small town—beyond the country club, at least.

When figure skating wasn't on TV, I'd go down to the basement of our little suburban house to practice my figure-skating routines—lining the walls of the room with cushions to create my very own rink, passing endless hours gliding around the room with the grace and ease of a yet-undiscovered Michelle Kwan.

From the outside, my carpet-skating routines were not actually quite as major as they felt inside my head, but they gave me something so important. Choreographing routines on my own in the basement for hours on end gave my imagination a place to roam free. Nobody was there to tell me how to move my body or what music was right for me to listen to. I could daydream about how if I nailed this short program I'd be heading into the long program in second place and could lock down my spot on the Olympic team. Being able to entertain yourself is a valuable skill, especially if you're in a prolonged dark space. (For me, that was Quincy.) Maybe that's dramatic and maybe I'm too sensitive, but there wasn't much naturally occurring joy in that era for me, so it was up to me to make my own. Especially being such a soft, round kid—who wanted to be a fit, sporty one—dancing made me feel graceful. It gave me a freedom I didn't have anywhere else.

Sometimes I even managed to get my two very heterosexual older brothers to participate. At one point, I insisted that in order to get better at my craft, I would need proper judges and critiques from my family, so I made these little index cards with a technical score side and an artistic impression side. I explained to Timofei and Boris and my mom that technical merit score comes from how nice your layback spin is, how clean your jumps are, how swift your footwork is, and artistic impression was more about how expressive you are with the music. When I dance to Mariah, do you feel it? (My mom was very cued in on figure skating, so she didn't need the explanation.) Once the index cards were ready to go, with their nationalities assigned—Timofei was typically the Ukrainian judge and Boris was a very tough Italian, while my mom liked to be a generous scoring Brit—we were ready to go. One time, my mom suggested that Timofei and Boris each do a routine to give me a little competition. I was shocked when both said yes. Timofei promptly improvised a dance to a Meatloaf song, where he had to do his axels as dunks with a minibasketball into a minibasketball hoop that he had installed at the top of the rink, because apparently this was the go-to method for butching up a potentially femme sports moment in my town. I scored him terribly because who does a fucking toe loop holding a GD basketball—am I right? And after that, I never let them judge my routines again. Fucking Meatloaf. But you know what? I think Timofei had fun. (Boris was so aghast by Timofei's performance that he could no longer take to the carpet-ice and had to withdraw from the competition.)

So it wasn't all bad for Jack. When commercials to support starving orphans in other countries came on in the middle of my *Power Rangers*—"For only twenty-five cents a day, you can keep one of these babies alive!"—I would think I was so lucky.

Looking back now, I think: how lucky I was to have a mom and auntie who allowed me to explore my ideas in femininity. Whether it was playing dress-up, my hilarious why-is-this-kid-asking-about-Madeleine-Albright questions, or wondering why my soft body didn't look like that Bowflex commercial, I had some supportive voices that many people like me wouldn't have ever had. My parents were raising a queer child in the midst of the AIDS crisis while they were both the age that I am now. I had terrible moments, but I also had moments of freedom and support to grow into who I am now. My father, too, for all of his shortcomings, has come the farthest. At my age, my dad already had three sons under the age of seven. The fear he had for his youngest son and the challenges this son was going to face in life, socially, emotionally, and in terms of health in the midst of the HIV/AIDS epidemic, was the impetus for so many of his actions. I'm sure a piece of it was how this would or could reflect on him as a parent, but I know the regret he feels for tearing me out of those evening gowns. I know he would do it differently if given the chance. The ups and downs of life have a way of softening your typical heterosexual man. My dad has come a really long way. As much as I have wanted him to be a more accepting or present father, he is still someone who knows me better than I wish he did, and has a sense of humor everyone falls in love with. My dad could be a dick, but he could also be lovely, and time has softened and taught him a lot. (I also, through twice-a-week accosting phone calls and relentless debates, got him to vote for Gary Johnson in 2016 instead of Trump, so my dad definitely has a heart.) But baby Jack, how little you knew about what you were in for, you little gorgeous queen.

CHAPTER 3

THE LOYAL TEA

AVING A NEWLY DIVORCED, WORKING MOM MEANT WE HAD THREE different babysitters. I loved Antonina, Darya, and Veronika so much, but I loved Veronika the most, because unlike Darya and Antonina she let me have the entire frozen burrito instead of just half, which were these gorgeous frozen burritos that were brown-paper-bag-material-wrapped, with a purple label for the bean and cheese, blue for the chimichanga, and red for the steak fajita, but I only had eyes for the bean and cheese purple-labeled one that I would place in this gorgeous oval-shaped casserole dish, and drown in half a bag of Kraft Mexican shredded cheese, then add two huge dollops of sour cream, a big scoop of salsa, and a Diet Coke on the side. Afternoon snack delight.

Occasionally, none of the babysitters were available, so my

mom would have to make us dinner, then take us back to the office, where she'd continue working until late at night or have a working Saturday moment. Sleeping bags under the desk realness. Running around a newspaper business after dark, it's a wonder my hand didn't get chopped off in the press machine. I was literally running wild. (Also, I definitely took my Rollerblades once and was blading all over the offices of the *Herald-Whig*.)

I loved the newsroom. She was hustle. She was bustle. Tons of men in midwestern newsroom suit attire: khakis and button-ups, probably from Sears—or worse, Joseph A. Bank, those pleated pants that make me physically ill to see. Not because they're ugly, but because they're just so gender conforming. But what I really lived for was the layout room, where they would be making the layouts for the next morning's paper. Precomputers, that meant a layout floor with cutting boards the size of a newspaper where they would meticulously cut and paste each page of the paper before running it through the printing press. There were darkrooms with photos hanging, still sticky with solution, under red lights, and a lady named Galina who ended up dying of a brain aneurysm when she was only forty-six. She had flaming red hair in a jaunty ponytail and smoked like a chimney and I was obsessed with her. Galina would come get me and keep me from bothering my mom, and we would stand in the darkroom together, her lifting me up so I could hang the pictures to develop. I also loved riding the back freight elevator—or as we called it, the "scary elevator," with a cage that you had to close yourself into. To this day, when I see an old elevator like that, my mom's voice comes into my head and I can hear her asking: "Are we going to take the *scary* elevator today?"

Really, the whole office looked like it was ripped out of a scene from *Mad Men*: It had old-school vending machines, sofas with vermouth-colored leather, corporate-looking boardrooms, and black-and-white-spotted marble stairs and the oldest revolving door in Illinois, which I thought was extremely special—until some jackass decided to have it removed. Why don't you just take a dump on this building's history while you're at it? I really loved that revolving door! As did a lot of other people in my town!

Beyond that, there wasn't much that made Quincy remarkable, other than the fact that the guy who dropped the bomb on Hiroshima was from Quincy. So was this golfer named D. A. Weibring. And Quincy played host to a debate between Abraham Lincoln and Stephen Douglas in 1854, which, mixed with a multitude of other events, ultimately led to Lincoln becoming president. Also, Steven Spielberg was rumored to have visited Quincy because his wife's aunt was married to a Quincy business owner! OMG, can you even? For many years, the World Free Fall Convention was held there, but so many people kept dying during the event's skydives that the insurance became too high to keep it going. Until it was canceled, it was the talk of the town: *The Today Show* came, honey! That was our claim to fame.

During the 1994 World Free Fall Convention, my mom called us from work. She was coming home and in a Helen-Hunt-in-*Twister*-level panic.

"Get up! Put on some clothes! We gotta go!" she yelled.

My brothers got up, too, looking bleary and confused. We all pulled on our neon Umbro shorts, high-top socks, and sneakers.

It was a muggy July day and already the midmorning was steaming. We stopped at the house next door, where my mom showed us the newspaper sitting on the doorstep. There, on the front page, was a photo taken of a guy who had been skydiving the previous day—only between his shorts, you could see one of his exposed testicles. Nobody had caught it. Now we had to retrieve every paper that had already been delivered. We spent the morning running all over town, scooping papers from front yards, holding them hostage until the reprint was finished.

A few testicle-printed papers might have fallen through the cracks, but somehow, nobody complained about indecency.

* * *

I saw the way my mom handled the shit out of the free-balling situation and I took that fierceness to heart. I wanted to be just like her. Even now, my mom and I are so alike. We look alike. We act alike. We both have a quick sense of humor. She can light up a room and, just as quickly, turn deadly serious. She's passionate, asks a lot of questions, and gets her hands dirty. If you're not putting in the level of intensity that my mom is, she will let you know.

I can see her now, at one of the T-ball games that I begrudgingly played in for one year. The other boys were wearing shorts, but I was wearing brightly colored gymnastics tights. And there was my mom, in an emerald-green high-waisted pencil skirt, a green-and-white vertical-striped blouse with big gold buttons, bright tangerine low-cut leather heels, ultrawide shoulders, and an ultrawide perm.

Because she was the daughter of the CEO of our family's company, she had to fight so hard to be taken seriously. People suspected nepotism, which meant she had to work twice as hard for half the respect, and double the hours without the title she deserved, even as she ran circles around people.

Before I quit Boy Scouts, I had wanted to hang out with the other boys—like Rustalav, who was heterosexual Sporty Spice, the best at soccer and pretty much the coolest boy's boy. He had invited all the other Boy Scouts from school over for a playdate except for me. My mom had to call and ask his mother, "Can

Jack come over?" It happened in front of me, and I remember so clearly how she had to make it seem like I had been welcome all along, and it wasn't weird that I was the only one who wasn't there.

She did such a good job of making it seem like things were always fine. No matter how persistent the bullying or frequent the social slightings and disappointments, my mom always tried to help me through it. She never made me feel weirder or worse about myself and I never ever had to question her love and acceptance of me on a human level. Which is something I feel like I must not ever take for granted. My mom accepted me completely when so many others couldn't.

My dad had called her "Padlock Mary," because she is a big fan of feeling safe and secure. After they got divorced, Mom would come grab us three boys for these family sleepovers where she would wedge a chair underneath her bedroom door to keep potential home intruders out. She loved having eighteen thousand locks on the door. Très *Panic Room* chic.

Could my mom's paranoia have come from the time I saved my friend Malvina's life? It was just me, Malvina, and a lemonade stand when a Jim-Carrey-in-*Ace-Ventura*-looking villain came walking down the street and told Malvina he had puppies at home and she could see them if she came with him. I stood up and pounded my hands on the table, sending lemonade Dixie cups flying everywhere. I started barking at him like a rabid dog. Then I started screaming for Malvina's mom. She came running out. "What the hell are you doing?" she screamed. He ran off. They called the police and ended up finding him on Main Street. Nobody was getting kidnapped on my watch.

Not to say that I'm a genius, but I literally remember their home phone number because I used to have to call to jump on their trampoline and play on their monkey bars every single day. Malvina taught me how to play American Gladiator on the monkey bars by swinging back and forth and trying to use our legs as claws to rip each other down. We also invented a fierce game where we would pull the trampoline below the roof and jump from the roof onto the trampoline into the swimming pool. We never got hurt until one fateful day when we were, like, "Oh my God, you know what would be great? Let's take this folding gymnastics mat, put it near the top of this extremely steep staircase in your circa-1800s house, lie on our stomachs on the mat, and zoom down the stairs. What could go wrong?" Well, the lip of the mat caught the edge of the stairs. We were airborne. What ended our rapid descent down the half-story fall was actually Malvina's wrist creating a cushion betwixt my skull and the wall behind me. As we crumpled to the ground, we were, like, "Oh, thank God we're not bleeding!" Until we looked down and saw what looked like an elbow sticking out of Malvina's wrist—a severe right angle where there shouldn't be one. "What in the Sam hell is going on here?" her mother shrieked as she came bounding around the corner. The crash had woken her up from a hard-core-REM-cycle midday nap. I was exiled from Malvina's house for all of six hours. It was devastating. But family friends are family friends, and we still totally had our graduation party together ten years later.

All to say, I didn't cause that much havoc. Who knew why my mom was so nervous?

Just like Mom, I also had an irrational fear of the I-70 killer from *Unsolved Mysteries*, the Unabomber, police sketches, and A-ha's "Take On Me" music video. Reader, it strikes me that maybe my family does have a deep-seated sense of anxiety that runs in our bones. Maybe it was that we were all sensing the inevitable collapse of print media and the pressure to roll our family business into something more productive.

But we found ways to have fun in the midst of all the stress. In the grocery store, we would play *Supermarket Sweep*, one of the most beloved game shows of the early '90s. "You have forty-five seconds to find the 2 percent milk!" my mom would say, and I'd be sprinting down the aisle in search of the refrigerated section.

Because my mom could make everything fun, I wanted her attention all the time. I would call from school and pull her out of meetings to talk on the phone, or tell her about the steal of round-trip tickets to Helsinki, Finland, I'd found out about from calling travel agents, or a sale on guinea pigs at the local pet store, or just that I'd forgotten something that she'd have to bring to me at school—my violin, or the clothes I needed for swim team. I'd run out to meet her at the car in front of the school and find the security officer scolding her for her irresponsible driving in a school zone.

My parents were committed to this gorgeous amicable divorce narrative, telling us kids that they'd gotten divorced for "grown-up reasons." It wasn't until I was sixteen, and in the peak of teenage angst, that I would find out the truth about what had caused the divorce: My mom had received an anonymous letter in the mail shortly before Christmas saying, *Honey*, and I'm paraphrasing here, *your husband is a damn skank who takes his side piece on business trips. He's been going down to the river and having a torrid affair with a tanning-bed-act, bad-perm-having, homewrecking bitch named Tashaya.*

Tashaya.

She was actually probably really nice and had just believed my dad's lies. As my uncle Pyeter said, nobody was in the bedroom besides those two—so don't make judgments. My dad was probably only being a skank at this time because he had been pressured into this marriage in the first place when he and my mom got knocked up. In the early '80s, if you made the choice to get preggers, then you were getting married. Or at least that was how it went in my family. Totally made for a thriving . . . divorce.

Mary wasn't having any of it. She bundled us up, took us to my uncle's, and put that divorce right in motion, while also shielding me and my brothers from the ugly parts.

Most of the ultradramatic stories I didn't hear about until much later. My most favorite of all time: My dad had moved out after the divorce and bought the smallest house on the block, just seven doors away from my mom's. It helped make his Wednesday night father-son time easier. It also gave her no distance from the drama.

My mom went out for happy hour for the first time post-divorce with her colleagues. She drove past my dad's house at about seven thirty on the way home from said happy hour because, you see, my mom was a fierce bitch and she didn't put up with no shit.

Lo and behold, she saw a car that belonged to another woman she knew in the driveway. (It wasn't even fucking *Tashaya*, mind you.) All the lights inside my dad's house were already off. At seven thirty! So much for his important midweek father-son time.

Unbeknownst to my six-year-old self, probably already passed out in a bunk bed after watching *Power Rangers* reruns, my mom straight up stop, dropped, and rolled out of the car. "Fuck it!" she said, as she opened up the front door to my dad's house to find him and his new girl in an intimate, half-naked embrace on the couch. My mom escorted this woman off the couch like a suitcase and threw her out, in her underwear, then went back inside and prevailed in a verbal assault that, while unhealthy, was necessary for my dad to see the scorn of a woman's broken heart.

The next morning, my mom woke up with a deep hailstorm-cloud-colored feeling in her heart. She couldn't believe that she had acted so barbarically. She realized that the woman she'd attacked was a manager at a local supermarket's flower store. When she arrived at the parking lot, she could deduce what car the woman drove because she could still see the handprints and streak marks on the driver's-side window as the woman had sped away for her life while my mom punched, smacked, and hacked at her car. Have I mentioned that Mary's a fierce bitch?

My mom strode into County Market with the poise and grace of Julia Roberts in the iconic black lace dress from *Pretty Woman*. She gave the woman a card, telling her that she'd had a couple drinks at happy hour and had lost her damn mind. And woman to woman—could she ever forgive her?

The woman obliged. They hugged it out. And a lady-on-lady trauma was healed.

Postdivorce, we couldn't afford to continue living in the house I'd grown up in, which was a '60s split-level modern moment—she was cute, but out of our price range—so my mom's parents said, "Let's swap." We moved into the house that my mom had grown up in, and my grandparents moved into our house. Que convenient!

We lived next door to Sabina and Borya: Sabina made gorgeous fudge, Borya had a gorgeous koi pond in his backyard, and Malvina Mikhailov lived down the street. I was thriving. When my dad came to pick us up for Wednesday night and every other weekend custody sessions, I would contort myself into all sorts of positions—like in an octagon end table, to disguise myself so my dad wouldn't be able to take me. Or I'd hide in the basement for as long as possible. I didn't love going to my dad's house. It just didn't feel like home. Mainly because he had terrible snacks.

After we'd moved into the new-old house, one afternoon we were out shopping at the local Kmart when my mom stopped the shopping cart and turned to face us. "I'm going to introduce you to my friend Steve," she said.

We got in the car and made exactly three turns—I remember it like yesterday, honey—down the streets of Quincy, past the house we lived in, pulled into a subdivision, and came to a stop. My mom rolled down the driver's-side window. The front door of the house opened and I saw a man approaching the car, dancing to the beat of "La Cucaracha," only there was no music. He did a step-touch, step-touch with his feet as he shimmied and gyrated in a salsa-style fashion toward the car. He was sunburnt shades of orange, red, and violet. You know the opaque light-blue-sky-colored gummy bear that's not translucent? She's kind of turquoise-jewelry colored? His shorts were that color. He was super bald, with wisps of bright blond hair, and very tall—six foot four. He was wearing a local basketball competition T-shirt, size XXL, and flip-flops.

He came up to the window and said, "Uhhhhhhhh, hi, boys." A long pause. "My name is Steve."

I hated him instantly.

After all, I had never been a fan of men in positions of authority. What reason did I have to be? They were always ripping me out of my gowns, tearing Barbies out of my hands, and telling me I wasn't allowed to express myself. It was basically *The Parent Trap*, and Steve was Meredith Blake, only I didn't have a twin.

Seven-year-old me had no idea that the man I just met was someone who would change the course of my life forevs.

Steve started spending more time with my mom, and pretty soon he was sleeping over. Which I now realize is false, as my mom sent me the following note when I had her read all of this to make sure she was comfortable with the level of disclosure in this book. This note is so hilarious I had to include it.

From my mom:

I have an issue with saying "Steve started sleeping over." Never once did he sleep over when you guys were in the house. He did insist, from a parenting perspective, that you stop sleeping in my room—he didn't think that was healthy for you.

So essentially all of that meant I wasn't allowed to sleep in my mom's room anymore, which was a big problem for me. At the time, there was this villain on *Days of Our Lives* who always wore this very dramatic pink-and-white suit, and she had come back from the dead. My brothers had made me watch the episode, and that old *Miami Vice* outfit-wearing monster had been haunting my dreams. She had icy blue eyes and was most definitely lying in wait beneath my bed, just waiting to slash my ankles, snatching away my chances at Olympic glory before killing me for my youthful skin. Sleeping next to my mom was the only way I felt safe. But now when I ran up to the door of my mom's bedroom from a nightmare, it would be locked.

"We're talking!" I'd hear my mom yell through the door. It took me until I was thirty to realize that "We're talking!" was actually code for doing adult horizontal bed choreography well beyond your young years. Which, gross! I'm glad they were getting their rocks off, but collective human trauma: Must our parents have sex? Accepting this reality is a level of wokeness I aspire to—knowing that your parents are sexual creatures and it's actually not gross. Just uncomf.

Back to my mom's email notes on the book. She says:

We did in the early evening, after dinner, go up to my room to "talk" or watch TV because you guys wanted to watch the TV in the family room.

Maybe Magdalena was haunting a day-nap dream, or it happened early evening. Thanks for fact-checking, Mom!

Anyway, as I later found out, Steve had been a very sought-after hot piece in his day. Ever since she could remember, my mom told me, she had a crush on a handsome boy with a wildly fun reputation, with blond hair and bright blue eyes and a sick body—he was a contender for the most popular boy in school. He went to University of Kansas, where he started to go a bit off course with some heavy alcohol use and questionable decisions. By the time he'd bought a bar back in Quincy, he hadn't quite become part of the cartel, but he didn't *not* let people sell drugs at the bar (which according to him was totally false and there was no drug dealing happening from his business, but it was definitely the rumor around town).

Finally he moved to the Virgin Islands to get sober, where he became Maureen O'Hara's house sitter and would eventually start the first AA chapter in a prison in the Virgin Islands. There's a blockbuster trilogy of novels' worth of material that Steve could write about this chapter of his life, but that story isn't mine to tell. Five years after, between Hurricane Hugo wiping the island out and Quincy being in the midst of the flood of 1993, which was massive, he had some property he needed to come back to salvage, so back to Quincy he came. My mom ran into him while they were out to dinner separately, creamed her pants since he was her lifelong crush, and the rest was history.

Even though he had a little potbelly and was more than half-way to becoming a bear, my mom still saw him the way she did when she was a little girl—the handsome jock who was the king of Quincy. (To be clear, "bear" is a big hairy gay man, and Steve wasn't gay, but that was the aesthetic.) They'd grown up two football fields away from each other; Steve had had a Jeep, and he was taking it around the block for a joyride when he saw my mom playing in her front yard. He took her for a ride around the block and she could still remember the way he looked that day, so athletic and all-American. Then, twenty-five years later, they ended up together.

This is clearly very sweet, but for me at the time, it was exhausting. I was pissed that someone was taking my mom's attention away from me.

* * *

For me, a young queer kid in Illinois in the early '90s, my mom was my confidante and safety blanket, and that blanket had been snatched out of my little gay hands. Then at my brother Boris's out-of-town soccer tournament, Steve came into the kids' hotel room and asked me if he could marry my mom. My heart sank. I lifted up my hands to cover my face like I'd just been called on *The Price Is Right* and acted really excited for Steve. "Yes, of course!" I said.

"I'm going to ask her tonight," he said. I was crushed. I realized that I would not be getting away from this person. In fact, I'd only be spending more time with him. And then an even more horrifying thought dawned on me: that I was no longer the be-all and end-all of my mom's universe.

As painful and confusing as it was to have my mom go from being my best friend to more of a traditional parent, I realize as an adult now that it was so necessary and healthy because their model of a secure and functioning relationship was and remains the main example of a healthy relationship I've ever seen. I've never seen two people be more for each other and in each other's corner. I've never heard one of them speak ill of the other. Their main goal was protecting their relationship in public and in private. There was nothing that Steve kept from my mom, and vice versa. And without that example, I don't think I would be a shade of the person I am now.

Steve worked very hard to soften the blow of their marriage and to win my affection. When the relentless bullying got to me, I would try to play hooky from school. I'd tell Steve, "I think I have a flu in my nose or something." Or I would complain of pains in my temple and eye socket. Really, I was trying to fake a migraine, like the ones I'd seen in Excedrin commercials, but I didn't know what they were.

"I'm sorry you're sick," Steve said sympathetically. "Want me to take you to the arcade?" I nodded.

At Aladdin's Castle, I'd run around and get tickets aplenty, working my way up to get that elusive Barbie Go-Kart that I was never going to accumulate enough tickets for. It was a mini Barbie-mobile; you couldn't fit in it, but your Barbie could.

After twenty minutes or so, Steve would say, "It seems like you're feeling a lot better, son. Let's take you to school." He did that to me three times before I figured out his trick. As irritating and rude as it was for Steve to dupe a helpless seven-year-old, I also realized nobody else from school got to go play gorgeous video games for twenty minutes during schooltime, so even though I had to go back, I got to go back with an endorphin surge, and I'd already chipped away an hour out of the school day, and it freed me up from having to truly commit to playing the role of sick because that's not good for anyone's day.

Meanwhile, in some ways my mom was thriving, but I also saw her struggling with disordered eating and her weight. Finding balance for her health did not come easily, and that affected me, too, since I was also out of control in so many ways.

When the surgeon general in the '50s came out and said that tobacco was bad for you, my grandfather went from smoking a pack a day to nothing. In one day. He quit cold turkey. My grandparents had lost their eldest son to a tragic car accident when he was only nineteen, when my mom was fourteen. They had a necessary rigidity and sense of duty to fulfill their prominent role in their town and to survive after being rocked by such a horrific tragedy. Not to mention my grandparents' generation grew up in the Depression and World War II and didn't have the ability to teach what they did not know. Self-care, self-love, and nurturing yourself were all considered hogwash. Just eat a balanced diet of a bottle of wine a night, a protein, a carb, and a vegetable, push your feelings down, and get on with it. So because they were dealing with that, my mom never had the space to learn how to care for herself. That cycle continued from my mom to me because of the extremely unfair gender constructs in her career and motherhood and life. It's no fault of hers—she's a hardworking, diligent, beautiful person who did the best she could and I honor her forever.

But I was desperate to find a sense of control and comfort anywhere I could. I had no healthy ways to self-soothe, so mostly I turned to food. I felt so much disconnection from my family, disconnection from myself, a general feeling of being out of place.

Besides, in a tiny midwestern town of thirty-six thousand people, where almost everyone else around me was eating to soothe themselves, too, it was something I could do in the same way, which made me a part of something, when I felt disconnected from everyone.

Meanwhile, Steve was still trying to connect with me. I was eight, and Mariah Carey and Boyz II Men's "One Sweet Day" was ruling the charts. It was the year of Mariah, honey. Her Christmas album had just come out, and she was everywhere. I had feelings to express about that number one smash hit.

Personally, I was stanning Dominique Dawes, whose showing at nationals that year was iconic—she swept all four ladies' events in gymnastics, on her way to the national all-around title. Steve had promised to help me build a DIY balance beam. It wasn't quite as dramatic as the kind my Olympians worked with: it was about four inches wide, and he built it from a splintery piece of lumber that he carefully sanded down, then attached a patch of thin light-blue Berber-style carpet around the length of the beam before nailing it to two little two-by-fours about three inches off the ground, making the top of the beam a total of five inches off the ground.

Once it was finished, I was ready to create my moment of moments. I began my process of choreographing what was to be, I was sure, the most beautiful, moving, and artistically accomplished balance beam set of all time. The mount to the routine was an off-ice-style single toe loop landed with one foot into a straddle-leap that then went into some side-step dance work that built into the apex of the bridge of the song—"And! I! Know! Eventually!"—I composed myself with two final hand rolls to the top of the beam to impress the Ukrainian judge (sitting to the right in my imagination). Then with dramatic flair, I turned my gaze back to the beam into a straight-on stance, with one toe pointed out in front of me, as I lowered my arms to my side with attention and panache, the likes of which had not been seen since Tatiana Gutsu in the '92 games, into the most technically perfect beam cartwheel, landing right on cue with Mariah's biggest belt. I successfully landed it only once in thousands of attempts. But my routine was three minutes and forty-two seconds—the exact length of "One Sweet Day."

A normal balance beam routine is only one minute, so obviously there were some dead moments in the set and a fair amount of repetition, but it was still stunning, and I set out with the best of intentions. I also broke a coffee table, smashed a window, and gave myself a black eye on more than one occasion. Most painfully this happened once when I was doing a patented Jack Van Ness dismount off the beam, but my knees bent in midair as I caught a fright, launching me, Molly Shannon in *Superstar*-style, into a pile of chairs my mom was using for a party.

Steve was most often willing to be my Ukrainian judge, my Chinese judge, and my Russian judge. The rest of my family was so exhausted by the '94 winter games that by the time the balance beam came around, they'd had it with me. But Steve helped me find my voice in my routine. You would think that would have begun to warm my seven-year-old gay heart, but alas, I found even less patience with him, because his heterosexual artistic tendencies didn't lend themselves to my creative movements in a way that really gelled.

But I couldn't figure out how to do any backward elements off the diving board. My Barani was sick. I could do front punches. I could do front layouts. I could do front pikes. But I was too afraid to do anything backward. I told Steve: "I'm too fat and too scared." "I can't do it." "I'm never gonna do it."

One day we were at the country club when Steve turned to me and announced, "Son, you're gonna do a back dive today. We're gonna get you over this."

I looked up at him, not believing him for a second. "Absolutely not," I said.

Steve's jam at the country club was to play golf, then go down to the men's locker room. He had been a triathlete, and now that he was sober, he tried to stay active. His triathlete body had left him years earlier, but his insistence on wearing Speedos had not. He would go to the clubhouse, and downstairs in the locker room, he'd put on the tiniest Speedo you've ever seen–no towel, no robe, nothing–just a little Speedo and goggles. He'd strut out to the pool so confidently–"Hey! How's it going?"–his body spilling everywhere, but so much charm. "Steve, you know I can't do backward stuff. I almost knocked your dentures out last time." Nevertheless, he persisted.

"You can do this," he said.

What gorgeous early exposure to body positivity. But all I could think about was how I wasn't going backward and how he'd lost his mind.

But this particular day, he got me out onto the diving board, standing behind me.

"I'm not going to do anything," he said gently. "I just want you to see what the beginning of the dive feels like." I walked to the edge of the board, looking back at him, the invisible unknown of the pool behind me.

"Put your hands up."

"I'm not ready!" I said. "Not yet."

"Damn it!" he said. And he put his hand under my lower back and forced me into a back bend and pushed me and finally, for the first time, I did a back dive.

It wasn't even that high. It was a one-meter, normal-ass diving board. It wasn't far to fall at all. But I was like, Oh my God, I didn't die.

When I went back up onto the diving board, I did a backflip into the pool on my first try.

And this, knowing that I could go backward, was the first step toward learning how to tumble. Realizing it wasn't impossible for me.

As a kid, I felt like I'd never get it.

Steve didn't know what he was doing for me, or what he was teaching me. He just couldn't listen to me complain about it for one more second. Nothing irritated Steve like a mental block. He was a man of action.

I wasn't like that. I got paralyzed by things. I'm pretty sure that "I hate uncertainty" was my first full sentence as a baby. So falling backward into something I couldn't see—that was the scariest thing of all.

* * *

So many of my best parts are rooted in my observations of my mom, Steve, and their relationship. Steve showed me how to be confident and proud in my body no matter my size. He believed that other people's opinions are not a reflection of you, as long as your spirit is thriving. My mom and Steve had an ability to always hold their individual needs, and the needs of their relationship, in the highest stead. Their need to love each other fully always outweighed anyone's need to be right. If I hadn't seen that with my own eyes, you wouldn't be reading this book. I don't know who that person would have become.

When I'm fiercely loyal, when I have the courage to trust even after that trust has been violated, when I can find hope and faith even when the world has given me every reason not to—that's the part of me that my mom and Steve nurtured. Even though I was a prickly, prickly rosebush, and she really wasn't easy to grow, they cared for me with so much patience—as much as they had for each other. That showed me what love is, and that it really can exist. It was the most hopeful lesson that they ever could have given me.

That day on the diving board, as he did on so many other days, Steve taught me to let go of my fear and try something new. All I had to lose was the moment, and a moment is something that we should never let go to waste.

CHAPTER 4

ROUNDOFF BACK HANDSPRING FULL

'D HAD IT WITH SCHOOL. ORGANIZATIONAL CUBBIES AS FAR AS THE EYE could see. Constant tornado warnings. Well, actually, just that one. And still, not enough closet space. I needed an escape. Not to mention there was Svetlana Vogenskaya. She had the nerve to steal my cousin who was my best friend and make her her best friend. Worse still: Each kid in the class got the chance to write the date, the number of day it was in the school year, and the weather on the whiteboard one morning. The order of which student got to write this information on the whiteboard with the coveted dry-erase markers was based on the alphabetical order of the student's last name. Which seems fair, but the kids at the beginning and the end of the roster got to go twice through the year because of ending and starting the list—get it? I could've gotten to write the date twice if only my last name was VUN NESS instead of VAN NESS. I couldn't stand how unfair it was.

School felt like a prison for my young, vibrant queer personality. I raised my hand. "Mrs. Plushenko, I need to go to the office and call my mom. I forgot my glasses again." Thank God Mrs. Plushenko was the coolest because she, unlike every other teacher I'd had prior and every other teacher I've had since, gave me no guff about forgetting things at home. You try being an eight-year-old violin-playing gymnastics-obsessed geode-collecting stamp connoisseur who has to have all those things with him in order to feel safe and nurtured. How else could I get through the daily barrage of insults that came from wearing an off-the-shoulder monochromatic purple sweat suit with purple Doc Martens. From an early age, I was all about shape.

Mrs. Plushenko nodded and off I went to the school office. There, I called my mom.

"Mom," I said, "I was dreaming about Shannon Miller all day and I can't focus. You have got to sign me up for gymnastics."

"Jack, stop calling me in the middle of class to talk about gymnastics!"

"But—"

"You've pulled me out of my third meeting this week to talk about gymnastics! We'll get you signed up."

"Okay, sorry, I love you, bye!" I said, hanging up.

Finally, I convinced her to let me join the Gymnastics Center in Quincy. Girls did an all-around practice, but there wasn't one for boys. All they had was that butched-up power tumbling troupe that performed at local basketball games. Power tumbling isn't an Olympic sport . . . yet it is a competitive sport. Some of the boys were really good—they'd be doing a punch-front-step-out-roundoff-back-handspring-double-full-twisting-layout-whipback-whipback-double-back-tuck. Some had wasted no time and were in gymnastics class early. Some were what the coaches called "backyard tumblers," because they were self-taught in their backyard.

None of them seemed gay, so no one I could relate to. They were rural country boys who just happened to do gymnastics. They would perform at the halftime show of the local university as a way to make gymnastics more locally on brand, and less scary and feminine for the townsfolk. Like, *gymnastics can be heteronormative and butch too!*

I assumed that I would be good right away. But as it turned out, I was kind of rotund, and not very strong.

Rurik Pavlovsky was our upbeat, jovial yet fit gymnastics coach. At practice, we'd do drills. I mostly worked on a triangle-shaped cushioned mat that you'd do back handsprings on, going downhill to make it easier. All of us were practicing when one boy yelled to me, "Your hair is really moppy."

"No, it's not!" I said defensively. "It's just curly!"

The boy in front of me turned around. "And you have buck-teeth."

"No, I don't!" I yelled.

A girl named Tashia Tomlovov, whose mother was another coach at the team, approached, with her mom in tow. "Boys, can you move out of the way?" Tashia's mom announced. We got out of the way for the Level-10s and elites training for the Olympics, watching them flex. One by one, they all did their gorgeous hard-core vaults. After the runway was cleared of the vaulters, it was the boys' turn to go on this minitrampoline run-way to practice flips into the foam pit.

The boy in front of me turned around and scowled at me. "Come on, fatso," he said. I watched him nail a roundoff back handspring layout.

It was my turn. I wasn't even close to doing backflips into the pit, so Rurik said, "Hey, buddy, let's practice our drop backs to backbends." I took a deep breath and fell into my backbend, but I had no muscle control. Rurik stepped in to grab me, then lost his balance trying to prevent disaster, and we fell into a heap.

When he made his way to his feet, he looked at me sternly. "Maybe for you, we just do backward rolls for now until we get your backbends a little better, okay?"

My face flushed. I heard the other kids laugh. I looked down at my feet.

I kept practicing and practicing, but with nobody who believed in me, and most seeing a huge target on my back with every move I made, the escape I was so desperately seeking vanished into thin air. Not long after, I quit.

All I wanted to do was twirl and tumble and cheer and move. How could I find my Amy Chow grace? Where was my Shannon Miller flight? I wanted to create the same visual excellence that I saw these powerful women executing, with moves so precise, so exacting, so focused. They were laser focused. It was something I've always known I could do if given the chance.

I also loved the sheer pageantry: I've always been obsessed with a special occasion, a big moment to get to look forward to. And the girls I wanted to be friends with, they all did gymnastics. I wanted their camaraderie, the way they were all part of the same team. Those girls would never make fun of me for making a shitty paper airplane. Who the fuck wants to make a paper airplane, anyway? I wanted to put on a leotard and spray a lot of hair spray on my bangs and curl them forward and then hair-spray them more and then put glitter on them. Why would you want to learn to start a fire with two sticks when you could be learning beam technique?

I never really cared about the male gymnasts, probably because I was so acutely aware of my own soft body. Watching men's gymnastics just reminded me of what I didn't have, and how I looked so different from them. With women's gymnastics, there wasn't that competition and comparing myself in that way—there was more of an admiration, a sense of looking up to them. The men made me feel self-conscious. The women never made me feel bad about myself.

Most of all, I loved how they had all the attention on them: an entire crowd riveted while you're so serious. I loved the drama of composing yourself on your fourth and final tumbling pass, dramatically bringing your arms down and you do that one last big inhale before you spring like Tom Cruise in *Vanilla Sky* down that floor.

* * *

In sixth grade, still looking to re-create that glamorous eleganza of Olympic pageantry, I decided to try out for the talent show with a lyrical interpretive dance that was never executed the same way twice to Jewel's "Pieces of You." I was excited to show my mom.

After I finished, it was silent in the basement, just the two of us. She sat on the edge of the couch so she could be face-to-face with me at my height. She held my hands.

"Jack, if you do this—if you try out with this—the kids will never let you live this down. They will always remember you for this. Are you sure you want to do this?"

Honey, she was serious as a heart attack.

"You will always be the boy who did this dance at the talent show."

"I know! It's a really good dance! It's so hard to make the talent show and this is totally gonna make it in!"

"I'll support you no matter what," she said. "But are you absolutely sure you wanna do this?"

Ew, lady! Yes! Look at this face! Did I stutter?

"Yes," I said. "I will attack this program with my double-toe single-loop combination!"

It was the first time that she had acknowledged to my face that she saw me being bullied already, and that something I was about to do might make it worse. She'd always given me room to be myself, to play with my Barbies and to wear tights. But when she made me aware that she knew what that was doing to my reputation, it sent the message that it meant something to her as well, and to our family. It wasn't conscious. She didn't do it on purpose. But this did not a secure baby Jack make. I didn't understand why she would care about anything other than what I wanted to share with the world. Or at least the hundred people in the auditorium.

And why would she? Nobody in my family really knew how to self-soothe. By the time I was in my early teens I had so much compounded trauma causing me to act out and reject authority from my parents. I wanted to numb out. I didn't have the vocabulary for the experiences I was having, which were all tied up in shame and sexuality.

It was confusing. My mom was in her own fight for professional validation and professional respect, which she had to work really hard for, and I respected that about her. Steve was a stay-at-home dad, so he was always attentive to me, but there were certain conversations I never wanted to have with either of them.

We didn't have tools, and nobody could give them to me. I thought sharing things was dangerous. As it turned out, I was right.

* * *

It started when my brother Boris walked in on me in the bathroom. I had discovered the art of bingeing and purging from a Lifetime movie that starred the actress who played the Pink Power Ranger and was called *Perfect Body*. I thought that was fierce and started to do it too—because who doesn't want to eat a whole box of Thin Mints and get away with it? It lasted for a couple years, until I finally stopped after I popped blood vessels in my eyeballs and gave myself a nosebleed, so it was really motivated by pure vanity. (Also, I started hating it.) My mom wanted me to go see her therapist, whose name was Dimitri Noranovich. I knew that Dimitri had been my mom's therapist since I was six. My mom had a few brushes of her own trauma—sometimes she would sleep for three days straight. Through therapy, medication, and the help of her psychiatrist weaning her off said medication, she'd gotten a handle on her mental health. I trusted him implicitly because of how he'd helped my mom.

Dimitri wore thin-rimmed glasses, khakis, and a button-up. His breath smelled like garlic powder and instant coffee.

I sat down and we began to talk about how I was fighting with my mom and having some issues at school. When I finished my monologue, his first question came so quick, it caught me off guard. "Have you ever been sexually abused?" he asked.

"What does that mean?" I said.

"Has anyone ever touched you in a way you didn't want?"

"I don't know what you're talking about," I said. I was genuinely confused.

"There's no need to get defensive," he said.

I hesitated. "If I tell you, you can't tell anyone, right?"

"Right," he said.

"I can tell you," I said again. "And you can't tell anyone?"

"That's right," he said.

So I told him the story of what had happened when I was kid—about the older boy who would take me into his room and play Doctor. I didn't have the words at the time to explain how it had made all those little synapses connect in my brain—because when something like that happens to you when you're at that young age, the connections between shame and sex, and the way we communicate about those subjects, is already so confusing.

I told Dimitri everything I could remember. Maybe the conversation in that hour meandered to other subjects too—it wasn't the only thing we talked about—but when I walked out of that room, I felt so much better. A weight had been lifted. I went home and went to bed. I slept soundly. I was sure I had done the right thing.

The next morning, I went to my first hour of English class and there was someone I had never seen before—a man in an official-looking suit standing right outside the class. I looked at him. *Huh*, I thought.

I sat down at my desk and pulled out my binder when the teacher came over to me. "Jack," he said softly. "We need you to come to the principal's office."

Instantly, I knew. *Fuck. Fuck. Fuck. This is not good.*

I went to the principal's office, where the dean of students was there. Calmly she told me that the boy who I had named to Dimitri the day before had been taken into custody. I leaned back in my chair and it made a loud, dull thud. My mouth was agape. My tongue felt like sandpaper. Time came to a standstill.

My mom met me at school and took me back to Dimitri's office. We passed a cemetery that I had passed ten thousand times before but it had never looked quite like that. We passed the high school stadium. It had never looked like that before. There was a film of gray over me, knowing that my mom knew the biggest secret that I had ever kept. When we'd talked about it when I was a little kid, it had been easy to write off as experimentation. Now that I had told an adult the full extent of what had really happened, it constituted abuse serious enough that the therapist had had to report it.

When we sat down with Dimitri, I could hardly speak. His office was on the first floor, with an open window covered by a screen. I stood up and ran to the window and kicked the screen out and leapt out the window. I ran through the parking lot into a cornfield and fell down as I was running.

My mom found me and brought me back to the car. My nose was bleeding. I was so embarrassed and ashamed.

"It's okay," she said. "It's all going to be okay."

"It's not going to be okay," I sobbed.

"We have to go to the Department of Child and Family Services," she said. She told me that she had talked to my aunt, who was a lawyer. *Great*, I thought—*now she knows too.*

"You can choose not to participate in this, and they won't have a case, and we can deal with this as a family in our own way," she said. "I'm not going to tell you what to do. If you want to do this, you can. But realize that if you do and there's a charge, it will be in our paper. Our family's paper."

My heart sank. "We love you no matter what," she said. "And it's your decision. But if you don't want this to be public, you just have to say, no matter how they ask you about it, that you choose not to participate in this because it would be detrimental to your mental health."

I nodded. And when they asked me about it, that was what I said. The only thing I said. Over and over again.

For weeks, they sent investigators to swim practice, trying to catch me being unsupervised. It didn't help that my family was well known in town, which probably made them even more eager to catch them in a lie. But because no one involved was willing to handle it through the Department of Child and Family Services, the case was dropped.

After the fact, privately, both families wanted me and the other boy to sit in a room and talk about it. I said no. In no world was I safe in that room. But it put me in another impossible position: it was either go through with that, or I would be seen as the difficult one again.

This was how I learned to turn everything against myself. It would take nine years of high-risk, self-destructive behavior before I would finally learn to take my toddler by his little curly head and let him know that he was okay.

* * *

We didn't talk about this stuff after it was over. But there were so many things that we didn't talk about. Steve was sober and my mom didn't drink, so if liquor disappeared from the cabinet, where did it go? If I left a questionable chat open on the computer and was asked what it was about, I'd say, "Nothing! Leave me alone!" and the conversation would stop there.

By the time the extent of the abuse came to light, the years of disconnect and miscommunication between my parents and me was a whitewater-rapids-level river—not crossable safely. At first, I was terrified that if I talked about it, it would be misconstrued as being my fault—that I had wanted it, or asked for it. I was convinced they would think that, and I had reason to be.

Because in my family, it was always my fault. I was dramatic. I was loud. I was clumsy. I was "out there." I was passionate. I was over the top, honey. This time, it really wasn't my fault. I couldn't allow myself to be in a room full of adults where that possibility was on the table.

The keeping of these secrets had created so much perceived acting-out behavior that came spilling out in all kinds of different ways that in my family I had garnered the title of what my therapist calls "the identified patient." Which is the person in a dysfunctional system who becomes the problem person by acting out the pain of the dysfunctional system. Which draws away attention from the true inner conflicts of the people in the system. I couldn't bear the pain of being the problem person anymore. I was determined to change the narrative.

Navigating through trauma, depression, and despair is a full-time job, which made it even more crucial that I found some light in the dark. I'm not sure what it is—if it's God-given, if it's my chemistry, if it's the nature or the nurture—but my whole life, becoming obsessed with something made me pass the time in all sorts of joyous ways. Honey, she has got to keep busy. By the time I was in eighth grade, I was ready to take on my next obsession conquest. I had shown rocks who was boss. I had learned everything there was about stamps. Coins—forget about it. I already had every penny made in America from 1889 to 1999. My collection was complete. I was ready to cheer.

So when Glafira Conradovich asked me on a dare to try out for junior varsity cheerleading, I was ready to make a splash.

Tryouts were fraught with tension. They were at the high school gymnasium—not the junior high—and there were at least a hundred girls there for ten varsity soccer spots, ten varsity football spots, six junior varsity football spots, and then twelve basketball spots. I couldn't tumble yet, so I didn't have to worry about those . . . yet.

I learned my chant and one-minute-long cheer with a diligence that hasn't been seen since Michelle Kwan's surprise come-from-behind win at the 2000 World Figure Skating Championships, and I approached every day of cheer tryouts with seriousness and earnestness because what started off as a joke was now my golden ticket to social belonging.

The day of tryouts came: Friday, May 10. I remember it like it was yesterday. And I gave it my absolute all. I left it all on the gym floor. I spirited to the judges with unparalleled enthusiasm. My exuberance and team spirit dazzled every single one of those hoes. But could they see past the social norms and gender constructs of this little cornfield town to appoint the first gay male cheerleader in Quincy's history? I went home drained. Spent. Exhausted. The seconds turned into minutes. The minutes turned into hours. The hours turned into days. And, bitch, that was just to get me to Monday morning. I had to somehow crawl my fourteen-year-old gay body through all day of school Monday with a quiet desperation.

We had to wait until Monday after school to see who made the coveted list.

When that final bell rang, I pushed kids out of my way with a George Costanza reckless abandon. I sprinted down the stairs to the hallway where the piece of paper was posted and held my breath until I found my student identification number—which I still remember by heart—typed on the list of junior varsity football. I was in.

The very next month, cheer camp ensued. That year at our fall homecoming pep rally, all four squads were coming together to do an epic routine. I was so excited to get to work with all the senior girls. Karlakov, our choreographer, who was much like the choreographer in *Bring It On* because he did essentially the same routine for all the local high schoolers but none of us knew, came in and gave us a drop-dead gorgeous routine. I myself—yours truly—had a fierce dance solo where all the girls squatted down but I popped up with a fierce "C'mon!" motion into choreography as the lyrics to The Offspring's "Pretty Fly (For a White Guy)" reached their chorus apex.

The season was really fun. We had eight games and I only had five beer bottles thrown at me. I only had "Faggot" spray-painted on our driveway twice. And only a 65 to 75 percent increase in people saying to screaming "Faggot," or "You fuck-ing faggot," or "Cocksucker faggot" at any given moment. So I would say my freshman year of cheer was really a success. But when football season was over, I had to go jump in that pool and start training for swim. I'd been swimming off and on since middle school, when I realized it could help me lose extra weight that was contributing to the bullying. But swimming didn't make my heart soar the way cheer did. My cheer fever was at scarlet highs.

I knew that I had to set my sights on being a year-round cheerleader, which meant that I had to learn to fling and flail my six-foot-one gay body with no core strength and hurl it into a roundoff back handspring in addition to a standing back handspring, which were the minimum requirements to try out for the basketball cheer squad. By the time football cheer wrapped in October, my goal was crystal clear. I had to be able to do a roundoff back handspring by the first week of May 2002 in order to make my high school cheer dreams a reality. This, of course, forced me to re-face my earlier failed gymnastics career, when Rurik made me feel I would never learn to tumble. But this time I had a newfound teenage swim-svelte strength (which we will get to later) and a new awareness of my body born from nine more years of self-taught trampoline and floor figure skating and imaginary Olympics competitions. Much of my childhood was spent feeling fat, eating pizzas, cookies, Pop-Tarts, and a smorgasbord of other delicious food to soothe the pain and discomfort I was feeling. This had a profound effect on my body image and my self-worth. It took me a long time to learn I was perfect just the way I was.

The difference between swim training and cheer training was passion. I was fortunate enough that Olga Valentinovna, a celebrated regional trainer—and the mother of local gymnastics superstar Tashia Tomlovov—took me on as a private client. So in addition to three nights of group tumbling classes a week, I also had two nights a week of private lessons to hone my skills as the first big gay basketball tumbling cheerleader in Quincy's herstory. But I was met with the cold hard reality that at six one, and −7 percent body muscle, learning to tumble was going to be a feat of physics that I was nowhere close to mastering.

By March, I had only progressed from the tumble track down to the foam floor—which is a far cry from the unforgiving no-spring thud of a gym floor—and the reality that I may not have my back handspring by the first week of May was causing me to cry myself to sleep on a nightly basis. And not a gentle cry. I'm talking you-just-saw-your-golden-retriever-get-murdered-in-front-of-you cry. Earth-shattering cries. Like when *The Great British Baking Show* moved from the BBC to Channel 4, costing me three of my closest friendships to Mary Berry, Mel, and Sue. But I knew that I had to keep going.

With the quiet determination of a five-day training regimen toward my roundoff back handspring greatness, I kept struggling. And kept facing that fear. And with each day I inched closer. And closer.

But you see, tryouts were on a wooden gym floor. There was no wooden gym floor in the gymnastics center. The closest simulation we could render was the vault runway, which was just a two-inch-thick piece of foam over concrete. By April, my Olympics floor routine was proficient enough for Olga to urge me onto the vaulting runway to start readying me for the actual tryout surface.

"Okay," I said. "I'm scared, but I'm gonna go for it."

I'll never forget the first time I threw my roundoff back handspring on that hard vault runway. Not realizing that engaging your core and squeezing your legs and butt together relieves the intense impact of landing your whole body on your wrists, I just launched my body upside down. The impact I felt from my wrists to the roof of my mouth to my hips to my lower back to my knees to my ankles was like jumping off a really tall bunk bed, when you get that pain so deeply achy in your heels you feel like you're gonna puke—it was like that. But the point was, I barreled my body into a back handspring on the vault runway, and I knew with a month to spare, I could refine this into a usable roundoff back handspring on a wooden floor.

There were bruises. There were twisted ankles. But there was a determination that existed only between my ears that was stronger than any bodily harm I encountered, queen.

Because there's only so many spots for basketball cheer—she's prestigious. There were sixteen total spots—eight for varsity, and eight for JV. And with this big-boned, large-and-in-charge gay girl in town with her roundoff back handspring, I wanted to let them know that the pressure for tryouts was fierce.

We were all practicing our routines at tryouts. "Hey, girls," I announced. "Let's go to the gym."

With the poise and dignity of Kerri Strug, I collected myself at the half-court line. Facing toward the hoop, I did a sashay-jump-run into the most gorgeous roundoff back handspring with a big ol' bounding rebound, just to let them know there was enough power for a few more at the end of that. And once I performed that gorgeous roundoff back handspring, I turned to see the girls with a shock on their face that I would not soon forget. I rode that shit all the way through tryouts right into a spot on the varsity football and soccer cheer squad, and the junior varsity basketball squad. But don't you roll your eyes at my JV experience—because we had a very competitive, deep field for basketball cheerleading, and no sophomores ever made varsity. Even though honestly, I probably should have. Because I was that good. Thanks, homophobes.

Rurik Pavlovsky had told seven-year-old Jack that he should stick with back rolls because he wasn't ready for back handsprings, and that had kept me away from gymnastics. But I'd finally found my way back to my love for something I'd been scared away from.

After I made the squad, Olga Valentinovna pulled me aside. Pride lit up her face. "Jack," she said. "I have never seen someone with less natural ability learn to tumble. You made that happen through sheer determination."

I had shown up for myself and accomplished something that I was convinced I'd never be able to do. And what's more, I was a part of a group for the first time after years of feeling alienated and disconnected from the people around me.

The part of me that's a cheerleader is a powerful one. She's endlessly resilient. She manifests things. She willed herself onto a hit TV show. She can find the silver lining when there's not even a playbook to begin with. When people ask me, "How are you so positive?" I never know how to respond. I think there is a piece that's nature, and there's a piece that's nurture, and in this case, I have a naturally tough-as-nails, Michelle-Kwan-esque part that just don't give up. No matter how many times I fall and fuck up my face trying to tumble.

Finally making the squad made it not matter so much that I'd been betrayed and bullied and that everyone called me a faggot.

When I was flying through the air, for the first time, I belonged.

* * *

As an adult, I was devastated when I found out about the culture of abuse in US gymnastics. To find out that so many of the girls I look up to have endured such harrowing ordeals is heartbreaking. Their courage and strength in bringing the conversation to light inspires me to speak about what has happened to me. It is unfair that abuse occurs, but the PTSD that occurs from the abuse is even more unfair, in addition to the host of behaviors we incur that stem from the abuse. It makes celebrating the joy and accomplishments of your life that happened anywhere near or around abuse harder. Speaking as a survivor of sexual abuse myself, I need to have my joys and accomplishments celebrated without feeling the weight of my abuse. The problem with that need is that it isn't always possible. Both my joy and accomplishments existed and so did the pain from my abuse. How can we feel one without the other? Joyful accomplishments exist next to painful memories. I found a lot of my healing when I realized that my suffering didn't undo my joy. So much of my childhood was painful, but there was also a lot of it that was beautiful and fulfilling and happened exactly as it was meant to happen. Survivors deserve to have self-expression, self-confidence, self-acceptance, and an unstigmatized view from society. Pervasive abuse continues to happen because there is a feeling that you can't talk about it because it is hard and uncomfortable to do so. But just like joy and pain coexist, so can discomfort and humor. Which is why you gotta buckle up, buttercup, because I can go from comedy to tragedy in three seconds flat. And that's not damaged or not normal. I hope culturally we can continue to normalize the idea that being a survivor is so much more common than anyone realizes and we all deserve to be heard, but more importantly are deserving of a recovery full of love, laughter, and light.

CHAPTER 5

LOVESTARVED

MY TEENAGE DREAM WAS SERVED ON THE PERFECTLY CHISELED, cold hard platter of Fyodor Orlov's lightly and rustically hairy pecs. It was never destined to be my pillow. I was never fated to safely rest my adolescent gay face on it in the way that I so desperately needed. He stirs haunting reminders within me to this day.

Okay, backing up. When I started swimming, I was in the seventh grade, and I was serving you five-foot-five, 195-pound realness. The swim teams were separated into levels, and all the boys in my age group were either in gold or platinum.

I had to start in bronze with the seven-year-olds.

There was one other girl my age who shared a similarly late start, and a lack of swimming ability. We were both just trying not to get laughed at by the small children.

How embarrassing to be arriving at four thirty in the afternoon to swim with the little kids when everyone my age was already leaving, because they'd gone straight after school. But what was I supposed to do? I wasn't a natural swimmer. I had B-cups and no idea how to move my feet quickly. This was a problem.

There was only one thing in the world I wanted, and it was to make it into the platinum group so I could spend more gorgeous time with the super cute boys and their lean swimmers' bodies.

The handsomest boy in the platinum group was Fyodor. Okay, maybe he wasn't the handsomest—that honor would probably go to Maks or Lukasz—but he was definitely a threat to the competition. If he could only have nailed down his evening wear competition, he could have been my Miss Universe. (And if only I could have nailed my swimsuit competition, I could have been his.) He was a natural swimmer, and the kind of guy who thrived under competition and pressure, whereas I was likelier to crumble. All Fyodor had to do was think about practicing and he would qualify for state. He was naturally talented, with a perfect swimmer's build, a gorgeous chest, with a little speckling of chest hair, and gigantic deltoids. He looked like he was on steroids, but he just came that way. He was such a gorgine specimen. An Adonis in our midst. The most Dorito-shaped hold-me-till-the-pain-goes-away then run-me-

over-in-your-car then resurrect-me-with-your-perfect-square-
shaped-yet-spherical-endlessly-hard-meat pecs I've ever seen.
My feelings for Fyodor are best explained by the number one
hit song "How Do I Live" by LeAnn Rimes.

In hindsight, he was pimply and had braces and was definitely a sixteen-year-old, but wow—I thought he was soy fucking hot.

As my ascension to swimming fiercedom progressed, I qual-
ified to be in the same group Fyodor was in, which meant we got
to spend more time together at weekend swim meets and daily
after-school practices. I would give every fiber of my young dis-
traught homosexual self if it meant I got to touch the back of
his toes at practice.

* * *

If Fyodor knew he was gay, he was never out; meanwhile, I was
never in. He insisted that he wasn't gay. That made it a deeply
fraught, weird relationship. To this day, we've never kissed, even
though we spent so many nights in the same bed. He wouldn't
come out to me until we were twenty-three, by which point we'd
all but lost touch. It gave me a bit of validation in myself that I
wasn't crazy, and happiness that Fyodor could live his truth and
tell me about it.

Back then it started with a series of awkward exchanges
where I would try to connect with him—my adolescent tits

heaving as I toweled myself off: "Hey, where'd you get your swim bag? I need one like that for practice too!"

"Oh," he said. "My mom got it made for me. I'll ask her. Call me later and I'll tell you where it's from."

Pretty soon I was calling him seventy-five times a week. This was before cell phones, of course, which meant I was sitting, sweaty-palmed, by my landline, dialing those numbers I knew by heart.

I got better at swimming, motivated by Fyodor, and also the desire to lose weight. When I left seventh grade, I was five foot four and one hundred and ninety pounds. When I came back for eighth grade, I was five eleven and weighed one-sixty.

Part of it was just natural, but also was me changing the way I ate and exercised. I wanted to look like the other boys, to turn those B-cups into pecs.

Fyodor was always nice to me. Out of all the boys at swim, he was the least ashamed to be my friend. When people made fun of me, he defended me. Of course, to him I was fair game—he would make fun of my chest, pushing my pecs with one finger, yelling, "Your boobs!"—but if anyone else did that kind of thing, it was game over for them.

One time, during Hell Week over Christmas break, when we had both early morning and afternoon practice, Fyodor took some of Steve's horny goat weed—which was kind of like Viagra, but herbal, and sold at gas stations—and ended up having to play sick because he had a boner for six hours. You can't swim with an erection like that. I didn't partake, because I knew better, and also because I didn't want to pry too deep into my mom and stepdad's sex life.

Fyodor and I were together all the time. Our lives merged. But even as we got closer, so much between us went unspoken. I wanted to be with him, and I was sure he was gay. Why wouldn't he just admit it? But at the same time, I was terrified that he would find out that I was in love with him.

I could settle for a kind of middle ground: being curious. I wanted to experiment.

It's such a precarious thing to grow up and learn about your sexuality. Even years later, now that he's fully out of the closet, I have feelings about it—like, even now he's never going to feel the way that I felt about him. That attraction just wasn't there. Now I'm confident enough that I assume everybody's going to be into me—how could someone not be attracted to me? (I'm kidding, but also not—I actually have developed a gorgeous delusional sense of self-esteem from all these trials and tribulations. But not adolescent baby Jack. She didn't have the range.)

* * *

One of my best girlfriends, Evgenia, who during middle school spent the school year in Quincy but summers in Las Vegas with her dad, had informed me that there was something called a "cattle call"—which was a mass audition to find America's next top superstar. I'm paraphrasing here, but that was the message that I got. She told me that these cattle calls happened a lot, and you never knew where you were going to run into an agent, so every time you go to the mall, you better be ready to serve looks. This could be the day that you become the next Britney fucking Spears. "Don't you know that a lot of people get discovered by getting dressed up and going to malls?" she said. I was gagged and knew then that I would never be half-assed when it came time for me to go to a mall.

So when Fyodor invited me to go to the mall with his parents while we were out of town at a swim meet, I said, "Of course. I just have to change my clothes in case there's a talent scout there."

"What?" he said.

"There could be talent scouts at the Springfield Mall!" I said. "I can't go like this!"

I went back to the hotel to change. I remember the outfit clear as day: a powder-blue Gap just-above-the-knee cargo short with a matching blue horizontal-striped sweatshirt, paired with a really gorgeous Birkenstock. I did my hair by putting a lot of gel in my fringe and letting the rest of it air-dry, because I wasn't sophisticated enough yet to know how to start putting product in the back of my hair. It made for a really crunchy, curly fringe, with everything else naturally dried.

I was ready to take the Springfield Mall by storm.

Maybe it was dumb of me to think I was going to get discovered there, but I was still savvier than Fyodor was. Fyodor wasn't the quickest, and I loved that about him. He wouldn't have known the capital of Missouri if it hit him in the face. His idea of a really chic weekend was going to his family's beach house in Branson to drink beer on the lake with his friends. That was never a destiny that your girl was going to hitch a ride on.

But I didn't really know that at the time. All I saw was how hot he was. And such a boy. The boys who I wanted to be with back then were all heterosexual (or so I thought), who probably had dingleberries and skid marks but, God, were they gorgeous.

Somewhere in him, Fyodor knew that I had feelings for him, and that must have made him feel good. But that was the manipulative part of the relationship that wasn't healthy for either of us: Me fighting for his affections. Him stringing me along so I would keep validating him.

I don't blame him. It couldn't have been easy for him either. I know it wasn't. He faced the same struggle of coming to terms with his sexuality and the expectations of his family and society telling him who he was supposed to be. Having the most aggressively-in-love-with-you, stars-in-his-eyes baby Jack nipping at your heels at every swim practice must have been hard. But we had mutual love for each other, and it was choked by the circumstances of the universe that were beyond our control. I can see that now that I'm an adult, and looking back, it negates every salty feeling I have toward him and his family. They were all actually really lovely people who gave me lots of really gorgeous memories. We were all just doing the best we could with what we knew, and I just didn't know very much back then.

So we made like gay Lewis and Clark and went on a sexual exploration. We tried watching porn together. Or we would walk around naked at the same time, which was really the sexiest thing we ever did. Or we would watch movies and cuddle—just shy of spooning. All that tension would build, but it never culminated in the way that I wanted it to. I've experienced it as an adult too—like when you're trying to figure out if you can suck your Uber driver's dick or not. I call it the forearm graze test. If your arms touch and the other person doesn't pull away, you can proceed with cuddling. If they pull away, you need to understand consent and accept that it's not going to happen.

We got drunk together for the first time, on Bacardi 151 and vodka, pounding shots. That night we definitely masturbated next to each other and then he threw up for two hours in my bathroom before his aunt came to pick us up and take us to Steak 'n Shake.

Then, to add to my agony, Fyodor went and got himself a girlfriend. I insisted on inviting myself to their dates, and then I would insist on buying dinner–"I got it!" I'd yell–just to make sure that I was as much a part of a relationship as both of them were. There were no boundaries. Very unhealthy. Very enmeshed.

We listened to burned CDs in the car: Evanescence and P!nk, "Cry Me a River" by Justin Timberlake, the *Moulin Rouge!* soundtrack, and Destiny's Child–the album with "Survivor" on it. And Avril Lavigne. Heavy Avril Lavigne.

I remember at our last state meet that we went to together, we had to shave our legs, and we got in the bathtub together to do it at the same time, bobbing in floating pools of nasty boy-leg hair. It was our last meet, because I wasn't going to qualify for state. We were fifteen. He had such a man-body–defined pecs and gorgeous abs and inexplicably tan for a white kid in the dead of January. (In retrospect, I'm pretty sure he went tanning–in fact, he definitely went to Sun Place Tanning in secret.)

But instead of trimming the hair and shaving it, Fyodor was seesawing it off, and hard, with dull razors, and blood was coming out as he was shaving. I grabbed the razor out of his hand. "That's not how you do it!" I said, and I showed him how to do it softly, gently.

And then we put on our cute little sweatpants and went

back into the bedroom and climbed into the bed we were sharing. It was a cold night, and I remember when I fell asleep in
that room, I already had stubble on my legs.

This was all I wanted—to be together and lie under blankets,
to creep on him in the locker room, where we were always dressing and undressing around each other. It was charged and felt
like a relationship, even though we never made out.

When he spent the night, we'd gradually remove items of
clothing. "I'll take off my shirt if you take off your shirt." And
then we'd both be shirtless. "I'll take off my pants if you take off
yours." And then we were just in our underwear.

"Let's go run around the cornfield in our underwear!"
And then when I came around the corner, he was completely
naked.

Oh my God, I thought. *Now what's gonna happen?*

We found a big hidden stash of *Playboy* magazines from
the '70s—hairy bush aplenty. We jerked off next to each other,
rained-on *Playboy*s in hand—talk about a budding young bro-
mance. I'd spoon him while we slept, then he would wake up
and yell, "You're on top of me!" and I'd retreat to my own corner of the bed.

When he got his driver's license, he got an '87 Datsun, but
his parents wouldn't let me ride in there alone with him because they thought I was too distracting and too loud. Which
was rude, annoying, and completely unfounded.

So we'd get into full-blown lovers' quarrels over the pettiest things—whether I was going to spend the night, or whether I was going to ride somewhere with him. But what enraged me most was when he was going to go hang out with some girl instead of me. One night, I was so furious I actually shoved him.

"You're fucking crazy!" he yelled.

"I don't care!" I said.

I was livid, because I didn't want him to date other people, but we weren't actually together. It was a huge pink elephant in the room.

"Oh, you gotta go on your date with Yelena, because if you don't have your alone time with her every week, then what will people think?" I said. I was losing my mind. "Oh, because your braces and your gelled hair are so hot, Fyodor! With your fucking old weird car!"

"I don't need this," he said. "I'm not doing this."

I chased him into the driveway, and he sped away. I had to turn back around and ask his mom to take me home.

But we always made up. The Sunday after Thanksgiving, we went out to get a Christmas tree with my family. "We'll drive together," he said. Nothing could have thrilled me more.

He let me wear his jacket and for a minute I felt like I was truly his. Out in this Christmas tree farm in the middle of nowhere in Illinois, taking cute pictures and playing hide-and-go-seek, it felt like we were a real couple.

By that point I was finally old enough to have my own friends, instead of going everywhere with my family, so we could go to the Pomona Diner and eat toast with gravy and nasty turkey and apple pie.

This is what the inside of my brain looked like: *When do I get to see you again? When's our next date? What's our next plan? When's our next mall trip? When's our next swim meet?* If there wasn't a next, I was not okay, and I would be calling him trying to figure out how to manifest one.

We weren't together. I knew we weren't together. He was straight, and I was the gay one. So I was incensed whenever anyone implied that he was gay, or that we might be together. I had to defend his heterosexuality, even though I didn't want him to be heterosexual.

Instead I escaped into fantasy, usually while listening to Christina Aguilera's *Stripped* album. In the raunchiest corners of my imagination, I would be in the locker room, towel-drying myself. "Beautiful" playing in the background. There would be a tap on my shoulder. It would be Fyodor. He would kiss me. "I'm gay," he would murmur. "And I do love you."

"I know!" I'd say. "I've known all along."

It didn't have to be in the locker room. In my fast-paced daydreaming teen brain, it could be anywhere from a bowling alley to Bali. The sweet nectar of the sheer thought of a reciprocal feeling was enough.

The year I turned sixteen, we went on a weekend vacation to Chicago with my mom. It was so gay—it was almost like we were trying on being a couple.

We went down escalators arm in arm. We shared a room without my mom that had two queen beds. We saw an older gay couple buying gay erotica at Barnes & Noble and started talking to them. They told us that they knew about people who got caught having sex in the restroom stall at Barnes & Noble and told us to be careful.

I couldn't believe that they mistook us for a real couple. Fyodor couldn't either.

"I'm straight!" he said defensively. I just gasped and tucked my boner into my waistband because I had immediately pitched a tent.

In hindsight I realize that older couple must have thought we were cruising them and mistaken us for being much older than we were, so they were giving us a warning about not getting caught doing the nasty in public bathrooms. Sisters helping sisters! But at the time, I didn't totally get it.

Maybe that was the beginning of the end—us spending weekends together, like it was too intimate to really last.

Not long after that, one day in the hallways between classes, Magdalina Steflikov stopped me. "I cannot believe you would tell people you and Fyodor are boyfriends!" she said.

"Who is saying that?" I said.

"You know!"

"I don't!" I said. "I don't know anything about that!"

It took two or three more conversations like that with our friend circle until someone finally said, "You told Varinka Prostokov you were having sex with Fyodor." But I had never told Varinka that we were sleeping together—I just said that I was in love with him.

I can't remember exactly how Fyodor told me we weren't going to talk anymore. Maybe he didn't even need to. I just understood that this was the new reality.

In one day, my life as I'd known it changed. My closest friends were no longer my closest friends. They believed the rumors and they did not believe me. I was no longer welcome at our little lunch table. The holder of all my hopes and dreams just bent over and took a huge shit right on them in such a callous way and I knew at that point that I couldn't live in Quincy with these people for two more years. I would have died first.

At the time it hurt me so deeply—it really turned me inside out. All these years later, looking back at the children we were, I realize that he never tried to hurt me.

But he did.

Much later, I would learn about how attachment is the root of all suffering. How desperately I needed to attach myself to him and how much I needed him to be something he wasn't. It wasn't because he had it out for me—but I couldn't know that at the time. I allowed myself to be hurt in that relationship as much as he hurt me. The power we assign to people is the power we give them—it wasn't organic to the relationship.

I had felt so happy and so complete with him, at least in certain moments, that losing him was acutely painful. Even now, as an adult, there are parts of me that still run from that experience, even if it ended up being the thing that helped start me on the journey from loneliness to a grateful solitude. From hating being alone to now loving my alone time, that evolution has been the most important to my well-being.

At that juncture, knowing that my competitive swimming journey was something I could no longer stomach and that cheer would get me a lot farther from Quincy, I was ready to veer off into my new direction. That meant spending only one more year in this town, getting as far away as I could, and sucking every dick I crossed in the process, honey.

She had been starved for affection and now she would no longer suffer rejection.

The amount of shame I had incurred at this point by being cast aside by Fyodor meant that I alone wasn't worth living for. I wasn't that interesting. I was too fat, too femme, too loud, and too unlovable. Now, according to the rumors believed by the people who I loved the most, I was a weird sex liar. That sent me on a many-years-long downward spiral of taking my inner child and beating him into corners.

I'd survived sexual abuse already. Now I was suffering the rejection of my closest friend. It left me with nothing left to lose.

Steve always told me: Son, you don't have to ride the elevator to the basement. That's a principle I've always tried to keep in my back pocket.

But Steve also always told me that every basement has a bottom. With a badly bruised ego and a broken heart, I was ready to make like Kelly Clarkson's sophomore album and break away.

CHAPTER 6

M Y CLOSEST FRIENDSHIPS HAD DISINTEGRATED. SWIM TEAM NO longer had my homosexual heart's desire. She was ready to break bad.

In the early internet age of gay.com and MapQuest, with an insatiable thirst for somebody who wouldn't reject me, I was off to the races.

I was young, lost, and reckless. And I was ready to make as many uninformed decisions with my body as humanly possible.

Not long ago, I was talking with my mom about all the pieces of my younger years that she didn't know about at the time, and I told her how much I wish I had not had to lie to her as a kid about where I was going and what I was doing. I wasn't able to be open with her and honor her as a parent, and as a result, I exposed myself to even more bad situations than I would have if I'd been able to be transparent. I learned to please my parents, instead of learning how to be a secure and functioning adult.

Becoming a secure and functioning adult? That was the farthest thing from my mind.

Since I couldn't open up to my parents, I had started looking for older men to explain to me what all this was. My gay urgings. My raging hormonal curiosities. I had more feelings and thoughts coming out of me than the mini powdered donut holes I had going in. And just like my obsession with donut holes, those feelings—I didn't know how to manage them. So I wanted to find a sexual sherpa(s) to guide me through this desolate sexual tundra I was in. That landed me in dingy apartments next to Super 8 motels, and a weird stranger's apartment who had a second cousin with a lazy eye out on the couch who kept knocking on the door really intrusively while I was trying to get out of my mind the fact that an old man made up of human soft-serve was hemming and hawing his nasty body into my supple young frame.

Those situations were truly traumatizing and not only tore pieces of my soul away, because I did things with my body for people that I regretted, but it also showed me the extent of pain that I was capable of numbing and sitting in. It wasn't until I was in my midtwenties that I started having sexual experiences that I was actually enriched from, instead of torn apart by. When

I fell in love for the first time, I learned what truly connected gorgeous sex was meant to feel like.

In the meantime, I was wild. Sex with strangers. Stealing my mom's car to drive to Springfield, Mapquest printouts blowing around in the back seat while I smoked a joint out the window. (I didn't have my driver's license yet.)

I also engaged in a lot of phone sex with guys I met in AOL chat rooms, which really helped me through the countdown until I could leave Quincy.

It was a weird limbo period, a mishmash of the innocent activities of my childhood and this dark, secret life—and me oscillating like a little horny baby between the two. You know how in the gym, you do a circuit of workouts? That's how my days were too—only my circuits went like this: Trampoline station. Donut on couch station. Chat room station. Phone sex station. Violin-practicing station. Cheerleading-chant station. Binge-eating station.

The phone sex station was ultramajor. You'd chat up someone in the Gay 20s or Gay 30s room and then jump on the line to give yourself a little hanky-panky. There was also a site called dudenudes.com, which was a very scrappy preporn site that gave me just enough content to get my rocks off.

In the chat rooms, I met a boy from Ohio, and we would listen to "Come Away with Me" by Norah Jones and talk for hours on the phone and have really intimate jerk-offs, and then, unusually, we would keep talking after, while we made our respective postcoital snacks. He was very involved in his high school's theater program, and he would complain about how unfair it was that the "straight boys" in theater auditioned for the same roles he did, but because he was so feminine he never got them.

We emailed each other pictures from school—chaste ones, never nude, and it would take actual hours to download those bloated jpegs on a dial-up connection. In one he sent me, he was dressed as Willy Wonka in a Halloween costume. It was my first experience with what I've come to recognize as a disease you can acquire from any man you're into: he shares something with you that causes such a knee-jerk ugh reaction that it turns you off him forever, and you can never quite shake it. The Willy Wonka thing was the beginning of that disease.

My parents couldn't figure out why our long-distance phone bills were so much higher than they used to be. "Who's this person in Ohio?" they asked me.

"Nobody!" I screamed. "Someone from camp!"

Which, like, sorry him! He was so cute and ginger. For all the times I've been hurt I did some hurting, and I hope he found himself a gorgeous adult life.

In doing a lot of the work I've done to heal the wounds inflicted on me in Quincy, I can see how in that era there was so much emphasis—both external and internal—on being who I needed to be for my parents, which happened to be the glaring opposite of everything I needed to be. My mom still accepted me completely and loved me all the way. Yet in the way that sometimes love just isn't enough, she couldn't teach me how to fully love and nurture and accept myself.

This may come as a shock, but I don't have a doctorate in parenting. I don't know what it's like to raise a child. But I know that when I was growing up, the emphasis was on fitting into the mold that was expected of you while under your parents' roof. You respect the rules and don't talk back. Once you're eighteen, you can do what you want. But if your parents pay the bills, they run the house. The emphasis is less on raising someone who can take care of themselves and more on following the ideas that have been passed down to you.

And then, suddenly, you're eighteen, and you've become a baby adult who's so angry and doesn't know how to self-soothe—you only know how to soothe your parents' nervous system.

What I needed to learn was how to get through a really painful experience of being bullied. How to deal with embarrassment. How to deal with feeling gross about myself. How to deal with extreme discontentment with my body image. But those weren't things that we talked about in our house. It was about following the rules, not about knowing how to move through life in a way where you could ask the question, "What's the next best decision for me?" I needed to learn how to become a more curious, well-rounded, independent person, the kind of queen who could work with other people but still be a ferocious bitch. Instead, I'd spent my life up until that point trying, and failing, to fit into roles that didn't fit me at all.

I was extraordinarily lucky in the sense that my family never kicked me out of the house. They were trying to manage the ramifications of raising a queer kid in a society where it wasn't acceptable to be queer at the time. It groomed me to be someone who really turned my discomfort inward and used it to hurt myself.

It came out in food. Tons and tons of food. In sex with strangers. In hours spent numbing out in chat rooms. In a super unhealthy relationship with my body. I didn't even know what healthy coping was.

If I'd known then what I know now, I would have told my little baby self that being strong and masculine has everything to do with having the courage and audacity to be different. It's such a better way to be a man—bold and courageous—than squashing it down and trying to fit into a very basic idea of how men are supposed to be. Not to mention that the concepts around masculinity are as tired as the day is long.

Not that I ever really had a chance of pulling that off.

Anyway, I was desperate to get out of Quincy. I was in so much pain from everything that had gone down with Fyodor—

especially on the heels of having my childhood sexual abuse nearly outed to my whole community—that I couldn't bear to stay in that town for my senior year of high school.

I set about finding other little forms of escape. When I got home from cheer practice at night, I would wake up my mom and Steve to let them know that I was home and safe, which was a rule in our house. The house was so big and creaky that every tiptoe you made would cause the whole house to lurch and groan, and one of our dogs might bark at any moment. Then, without starting the car at the top of the driveway, I'd put that shit in neutral so it didn't make a peep, and push it to the edge of the street before giving her a start.

I had new friends, honey, and they were dangerous. They smoked weed. They broke curfew. We were Bad Girls.

With my new girls—Karina, Andreja, Elina, and Helenka—we drove around to gas stations until we found one that would sell us booze and cigarettes, then go to buy a dime bag of weed so we could roll a B and hit a route. We listened to Usher, went through the Taco Bell drive-thru, and embraced our *Sisterhood of the Traveling Pants* bad bitch journey.

That year, it came time for my family to make our annual trip to our cabin on the Upper Peninsula of Michigan. It was a fifteen-hour drive from Quincy. We weren't going to the mitten of Michigan—we were going all the way up to the fingertip attached to Wisconsin.

In the car, we'd play games. One of my favorites we called "The Cow Game"—dividing the car down the middle, and however many cows were off grazing in the fields on the side of the car you were seated on would up your total cow count. But if your side of the car drove past a cemetery, all your cows would be wiped out, and if you drove by a farm that had a white horse, you'd triple your count. My grandfather, in an eternal effort to never lose, knew every landmark on those roads, so he would reroute us, and the trip would end up taking eighteen hours as we avoided cemeteries and drove past every white-horsed farm.

But when we took this trip the year I was sixteen, I was already starting to unravel. I didn't yet know how to roll my own blunts, so my girlfriends had rolled me four or five, which I'd stuffed into my pack of Newport Light 100s. It was hard to come by cigarettes—I'd have to go to, like, eight gas stations to not get carded. On the way up, I smoked half a cigarette, then stubbed it out and put it back in my pack. They were too precious to waste!

At the cabin, I loved to wake up and pour myself a big bowl of Cinnamon Toast Crunch, then go outside and smoke half a blunt and eat my cereal while the sun came up. A beautiful Bob Ross meets a stoner General Mills moment.

Driving back from the cabin at the end of the trip, we stopped off at a gas station, and I realized I still had a stale half cigarette in my pack, so I smoked it. It tasted gross after collecting dust in my pack for a couple days, but I kept powering through it. After all, I'm no quitter. I washed my hands and drank some water after, but I still felt queasy.

On the way back, I was in the back of the car, starting to feel more and more nauseated. I could taste it from the back of my throat to the tip of my toes, from a foot outside my hands all the way into my pee-hole. I had become the stale half Newport Light 100. The edges of my lips felt like they were turning the same mint-green color of the box. I was so sick. But I couldn't tell my mom and Steve that I had started smoking cigarettes—they could never know.

I felt it rise up in my throat and, uncontrollably, I began to puke all over myself. There was no bag to deposit it into, so I just puked on my shirt.

"Jack, what's wrong?" my mom said.

"I'm sick," I gagged.

We pulled over to another gas station and I changed clothes, throwing the other outfit away.

The next day, I went to smoke weed with my friends at a cornfield we always went to called Roller Coaster Road. We'd smoke, listen to music, and hang out. I had Annie Lennox's "Walking on Broken Glass" on repeat and we were dancing around, playing a game called Elevator where you would crouch down and take a few calming breaths, then the giver of the elevator would take a smoking blunt, burning side in their mouth, and blow into your mouth as you stand up. My poor brain, I'm so sorry for the ways I've hurt you.

As I reached the apex of my elevator, I felt a swarm of bees inside my head. It was the last thing I felt before I passed out. My friends told me later that I just fell to my knees and collapsed, then rolled over stiff as a board. Like I imagine Alexander Hamilton dropping to his knees as he was killed. In the process, I fucked up my face hitting the ground.

When I came to, my phone was ringing. It was my mom.

"Come home," she said. "Right now." It was clear from her voice she wasn't playing around.

"Mommy, I can't," I said. "I'm still at cheer."

"Cheer's over!" she said. "You're not at cheer!"

"Tryouts are in a month and a half!" I said. "I am at cheer!"

"Come home right now or I'm reporting your car stolen," she said. "We know about your heroin! We found the spoon and the lighter! Oprah was just talking about how to tell if your child is on heroin!"

As it turned out, I had left a spoon from my Cinnamon Toast Crunch and a lighter out on the back patio at the cabin. Shit.

"Mom, you're fucking crazy," I said. "I'm not coming home."

"Explain the spoon and the lighter, then!"

"I was eating Cinnamon Toast Crunch on the balcony!"

"I'm calling the police!" my mom said.

I wish I'd been able to have a real conversation with my mom about how I was using marijuana—that I needed it to cope with my anxiety, with living in Quincy, with feeling so hopeless and misunderstood.

Steve was always instrumental in that—being able to talk my mom down after she saw "Five Things You Should Know About Teenage Drug Use" clips on *Oprah* and started checking the screens inside all the faucets to make sure they hadn't been taken out. (If there were no screens in your faucets, your teens were using them to smoke any multitude of drugs.)

Back at home—and freshly conscious after passing out in a cornfield, so obviously, *totally* fine—we talked it out. "Mary," Steve said patiently, "if he was on heroin, he would have track marks and bruising."

I ended up coming clean about the cigarettes, explaining that that was why I was vomiting all over myself—not heroin withdrawal. That made a lot more sense to them.

It was classic Steve: knowing how to deescalate, and be that force of calm and good.

Not long after that, Steve walked out to the driveway and caught me in the family Jeep deeply receiving a guy I'd been dating. He looked at us, quietly said, "Boys, it's time for Jack to come inside," and just walked back into the house.

When I came inside, Steve was already in bed with the lights out. Classic Steve.

I was hell-bent on getting out of Quincy and graduating early and bit by bit, I wore away at my parents' resistance. I took away every reason they had to say no.

The requirement to get extra credits in order to graduate early? I got 'em. The college cheer squad that you needed to make to leave early? Made it! The ACT score to get accepted? Nailed that shit too. Through every ounce of my mom's apprehension, I bulldozed my little body out of Quincy, Illinois.

I've always had a little bit of a *Sliding Doors* curiosity about what would have happened if I'd ended up at a different school. I tried out for cheer squads at University of Colorado-Boulder, University of Arizona, and University of Illinois-Chicago. But my dad went to Arizona, and I'd been to visit his parents in Scottsdale, and when I was a sophomore in high school, we went to Tucson to see the school in real life, so it was familiar to me. I knew I'd be comfortable there. Meanwhile, Colorado was where JonBenét Ramsey was killed, so that was out—even though I made that squad too.

So I was off to Tucson to make a big splash. Training for cheerleading in college was a whole different animal. It was twice-a-day practices, cheering at four games a week—we did volleyball, football, and basketball—so it was a lot busier, and we had to cover both men's and women's. I also took fifteen hours of classes a week my first semester because I wanted to stay busy. But I quickly realized that watching old episodes of

Golden Girls and *The Nanny* on Lifetime in my dorm room was much more fun than going to astronomy (which I had confused with astrology—I couldn't believe I didn't get to learn about the zodiac, and instead was subjected to pure math).

In astronomy class, I sat next to a girl named Sofiya, who was despondent every day and feeling like she had no friends in college. I swooped in for the rescue. She asked if I knew anyone who had weed.

"Duh," I said. Pointing to myself, "This little girl, and in my back pocket."

I gave her a joint and continued about my day. That night, returning from a problematic sexual encounter, there were ten University of Arizona Police Department cars outside my dorm. To the crowd of onlookers gathered outside, I said, "Oh my God—who's in trouble?"

At that moment, a group of police officers approached me and asked if I was Jack Van Ness.

Oh God, I thought. "Uh-huh. I am."

They took me around a corner and showed me a camera that had pictures of Sofiya rolling a joint and smoking it in her dorm room as she took selfies. They told me Sofiya had been caught smoking marijuana in her dorm room and that she had informed them that I was a supplier. They had already searched my room but hadn't found anything—now they had to search my car.

"My friend Doroteya has the car," I said. Doroteya was a girl I had met at my first gay party two weeks prior and, in typical healthy gay boundaried fashion, we immediately became best friends, so I gave her the keys to my car and she drove me around, and then used the car at her leisure all the other times, because why not? She was my best friend now!

I continued to refuse the car search for the week, at which point I received a letter saying that while I wouldn't be charged with any criminal proceedings, I was being evicted from campus housing because I'd had knowledge of a controlled substance on campus and hadn't reported it.

My mom was furious. I prayed to the thirteen goddesses that the cheerleaders wouldn't find out. I had already inexplicably passed a drug test—that I had been certain I would fail—so I had come too far to relinquish my spot on the squad now.

So I cheered my way through the first semester all the way to a 1.7 GPA. I told my parents I had a 3.5. "Everything's going great!" I assured them as I hopped back on the plane to go back for my second semester.

Then came the unfortunate task of having to call my parents to let them know that I was kicked off the cheer squad for my low GPA and would have to retake the astronomy class from the term before because I'd been caught cheating (with Sofiya, who I hadn't learned any lessons about from weed-gate, so we decided to try to cheat on our final together and both got caught).

So naturally, because my mom had been cool and allowed me to manipulate her into getting me and Doroteya a one-bedroom, one-bath apartment just off campus so I could continue to pursue my downward spiral of a second semester, I quickly met a local pimp named Bogdan on Gay.com in January.

I told him I was in dire financial straits and had just dropped out of college. My parents would pay for my rent, as they were on the lease, but car payments, phone, and living money was on me now. Not to mention, how I was going to afford the party-life necessities of marijuana, cocaine, alcohol, and all the other balanced needs of newly eighteen-year-old me. This was the only way I saw to go forward, and how bad could it be?

Bogdan gave me my first escort bag. It contained a burner phone, condoms, and pepper spray, in case a john ever got too physical. Bogdan was really nice in the sense that he made sure to tell me about the dangers of unprotected sex and let me pay my 50 percent commission for the johns he found through sexual favors to him directly for the first two months. I was swimming in the dough. Doroteya and I were serving Scarface ferosh and I only spent six hours a day shaking, naked, and crying in the corner of our shared bedroom.

I was thriving.

I understand that this is probably très jarring to read. But the reality is that LGBTQ+ people face challenges at disproportionately higher rates than their straight counterparts—drug use, sex work, and financial instability can be an unfortunate result. My privilege as a young cis white man whose parents weren't going to let me drown afforded me the ability to make those mistakes and live to talk about it. I was also lucky that I was resilient by nature, having already been hardened enough by my experiences in Quincy that I could survive this too.

Still, this is particularly painful for me to write about. Even deciding how to share this was incredibly difficult. When I was a little boy in a lot of pain and confusion, I used to think that I wanted to help other kids who were going through it like me. I imagined starting a really chic wellness center for other lost gay babies–in my head it was an A-frame log cabin–that would have a juice bar and a yoga studio with really bomb scones and healthy snacks, and probably a spa room once we expanded and started to franchise it out. I never thought I'd be sharing it this way.

But we have to talk about these subjects, and take them out of the shadows. Which is why I'm doing this–because I hope that speaking my truth might help other little baby Jacks not have to make some of the really hurtful, traumatic mistakes I made. Because a lot of other little baby Jacks never lived to tell their stories.

So here we go. Soon, Bogdan started wanting to collect his half of the funds, so he sent me to what was, unbeknownst to me, an active meth house. Doroteya would always drop me off at my jobs to make sure that I didn't end up on a missing persons list. She would drop me off, roll a few houses down, and sit and wait for me to come out. Approaching this house, I knew that something was off. I entered the front door and there was a toothless man who had a smoky lavender hue to his ashy-skinned body. He invited me to the couch that he sat on, pulled out a gigantic bong full of what I now know was meth—I didn't know what it was then—and asked me if I partied. I said no.

Just then I heard the sound of three other men coming in from the back of the house. Their energy was not one I was curious to investigate further if I planned to keep all my limbs attached to my body. I asked my client if we could be excused to his bedroom. He obliged.

In his bedroom, he closed the door and turned and looked at me. "I was a guy like you, once," he said. "Here's your cash. I know how important this is." He put it on the dresser.

"I won't kiss," I blurted out. "Only handjobs. That's all I'm comfortable doing."

"Okay," he said. "I understand. This house is kind of scary."

"Yeah," I said. "It is."

He sat down on the bed. "Well, I'm actually moving to Mexico tomorrow," he said. "I've been running from some things for some time."

He reached under the bed and pulled out a black box. Out of the black box he pulled out a gun.

I registered that my top was already off and my shoes were at the front door. All I had was my escort bag. The envelope was directly within reach on the dresser.

In a split second, I made the quick decision to grab the envelope, turn around, and do a dive-roll out an open window. Realizing that there was a screen, but with no time to waste, I burst directly through the screen onto the dusty red clay front yard and ran for my life to the car waiting a few blocks ahead.

I called my mom the next day, crying so hard almost no noise could come out. I told her I had been selling my body and I had to come home.

"What does that mean?" she asked.

"What do you think it means?" I said. "I'm selling my body! Your kid is selling his body!"

My mom said she would transfer me five hundred dollars the next day and that I could come home.

In the midst of my escorting months I had found a little black kitten under the hood of a car early one morning with Doroteya when we were up to no good. I brought that cat home and every night I would sleep with him out on the couch because Doroteya would be in our one bedroom in this filthy apartment, and I would think, *I've gotta get this little kitten out of here.* I called him Bug, because he was such a little lovebug. (In truth, his original name was Jayden, but after Britney Spears decided to name her son that as well, I knew that my cat and

Britney Spears's son couldn't have the same name. Not that there's anything wrong with sharing a name with Jayden Spears. It was just a little too human for me.)

So I packed up Bug in my brother's hand-me-down Jeep, with all my worldly possessions. I'd have to figure out a way to smuggle Bug into my mom's house and parlay this devastating experience of college humiliation into a new track in beauty school.

No matter how ugly everything had gotten, I was still convinced I could find a way to make it gorgeous.

CHAPTER 7

GUTSY QUEEN

BACK IN QUINCY, I GATHERED MY BEARINGS. I'D ONLY MADE IT through one semester of college, plus another two weeks of my second term—just long enough that we couldn't get the tuition refunded. Sort of like Nastia Liukin's comeback in 2012 at the Olympic Team Trials. She knew she had something to add to the team with her skills on uneven bars, but in the middle of her routine, she literally belly flopped from the highest of heights. In that moment she had to make a decision: she could lie there and then slink off that competition floor—or she could jump back on the bars, nail that dismount, and be the Olympic champion queen that she is. Would she make it to the team? Absolutely not! Márta Károlyi would never stand for that. But the point is: Nastia finished with dignity and grace. And so would I. (Except I wasn't an Olympic champion. I had flunked out of University of Arizona with a 1.7 GPA after turning tricks. But my spirit remained indomitable.)

When I arrived home, my dad asked if I wanted to meet him for a bite to eat. As I did my best Tyra Banks power-stomp into the local sports bar, trying to give myself a little pick-me-up, I looked up to see my dad was fuming. "I'm so mad at you, I could hit you," he said.

"Do it, old man!" I said.

He actually backhanded me across the face.

Everyone was mad at me. I was mad at me too. I had gone and proved my parents right, that I had been too young to leave, and just did a face-plant with nothing but a tiny beautiful kitten to show for it. My next move would determine everything. It was clear that I wasn't cut out for a life of academia. But I also knew that I needed a path forward. I didn't want selling my body to be how I supported myself. I have no judgment of sex workers—there are so many different reasons why people choose that work—but personally, it put my soul into a blender. I didn't protect myself. I wasn't thriving. It didn't make me feel good.

If college was the US figure-skating championships, I had fallen on every single jump, tripped on my toe pick and landed on my face, and succumbed to my nerves all over the ice. Now I had stopped training because I'd broken my kneecaps in my last and final jump—and had to move back home devastated and medal-less.

So I snuck Bug into my mom and Steve's house and took a job helping out at the family paper to make some money while I figured out my next steps. I had come back, tail between my legs, to a place I had spent so long trying to escape from. Now I saw what my life would be like if I stayed in Quincy and worked at the family business. It was a nonstarter.

* * *

A big part of me had always wanted to go to hair school—ever since I was a little kid, trying to zhuzh up everyone around me. But I wasn't even sure if I would really like it, or if doing hair was just a gay stereotype. I was putting all my eggs into a basket that I didn't know I was going to love—just because I thought it was fun to color my own hair in high school? Besides, there was that time I turned poor Varinka Prostokov's hair fire-engine red by accident. What if this was another dead end?

My family said I'd have to pay for hair school myself after the failed Arizona experiment. So with a dream in my pocket and a FAFSA application, off I went.

I decided to go to the Aveda Institute in Minneapolis, since it seemed like a cool city, and moved into a tiny apartment across from a 7-Eleven.

It was an eleven-month program, which came out to sixteen hundred hours of study. It was an opportunity for me to make new friends and reinvent myself. It was there that I started going by Jonathan instead of Jack. The student body was diverse—a lot of blondes from the Midwest, but also a lot of Somali women, since Minnesota had been the only state to take in Somali refugees. I was surprised by the diversity of Minneapolis, and being close to downtown and right down the road from University of Minnesota, we had students from everywhere, we had business people, homeless people. We were in a position to learn how to do hair on so many different types of people. They expanded my worldview as well as my hair skills. Not long after we started to study, I was working with textured hair on women of color, so that never intimidated me. Our textured hair teacher, Hethersova, was a passionate educator of all things hair and also a woman of color. Our first day of textured hair class she let us know we would be doing relaxers, braids, reformation curls, and not to be scared of hair on people who don't look like you. Hair is hair, she would say, it's our job to learn how our tools manipulate the hair. I'm so grateful for that experience early on in my career because I have seen some hard-core fixes come in and out of my chair, and those early days prepared me well.

That time at Aveda was what ignited my passion for ingredients and started my understanding of how they can affect our body differently. When you put naturally derived ingredients like an aloe, an essential oil, or a dehydrated quinoa powder on your body, skin, or hair, the way they react is completely different from how synthetic ones do. As someone who had previously only worked with powder in the form of tiny donuts or cocaine, this was enlightening.

Aveda was derived from ayurveda, which is a form of Eastern medicine based on preventing illness as opposed to treating it. I fell in love with Aveda's sustainably sourced products and natural ingredients. Once Estée Lauder acquired Aveda, what was once in glass jars became something that felt much slicker, but still, I drank the Aveda Kool-Aid. I was never going to work anywhere that wasn't Aveda. I became an Aveda girl, through and through.

I couldn't only go to school, though—I still had to work. First I got a job as a server at Applebee's, but I wasn't very good at it. People ordered chicken fingers and I'd bring them back chicken fajitas. If they ordered a Sprite, I'd bring them a Coke. I wouldn't let them send it back because then my manager would know I'd fucked up the order. "Please just don't complain," I'd whisper to the table. "I don't want to get fired. I just don't know how to work the computers and I'm super stressed out." I was way more concerned about keeping my naturally curly hair flat-ironed than I was with getting your order right. My first shift, I had twelve comped meals out of my fifteen tables.

I lived on about $17 a day, scraps of uneaten Applebee's food, and Nutter Butters, until I got fired after only three weeks.

Next I got a job at a restaurant in downtown Minneapolis. On my first day, I had written down a message on the back of one of the business cards that were stacked at the host's stand. The manager who was training me took me aside. "Never ever write on a business card," he said. "They're very expensive. It's a waste of cards."

I nodded. He seemed very serious about this.

The next day, an old heterosexual walked up to be seated just as I was finishing a call with a customer. I was looking for a scrap of paper to take the message on for the person who had called, and I didn't want to waste a business card after having been chastised for it the day before. Helpless, I ended up taking a pen and writing the message down on my hand.

The old heterosexual at the host's stand, waiting for his table, looked at me like I was crazy. He picked up a business card. "Why don't you write on this?"

"No!" I said. "I can't!"

I went to seat the people in front of him and when I came back, he was still standing there, irritated. "Can I speak with you?" he said.

It turned out he was the owner of the restaurant.

He pulled me back to the kitchen and chewed me out in front of the entire waitstaff and all the cooks. "You know what?" he said. "If I wanted advice on how to take messages from a host with a Flock of Seagulls haircut who wears bowling shoes with khakis, I'd ask for it! But I didn't ask for your advice, because I own this fucking restaurant!"

I ran out, flustered. My manager called me after and apologized, but the damage was already done. "I'm never coming back!" I cried on the phone.

Instead, I befriended a girl named Daniilushka who sent all her friends to be my clients in hair school. They only had to pay $12 for the haircut, and then they would tip me $10, which gave me just enough money to live on.

That year at the Aveda Institute, I ran for student council president and won. But after I took office, this girl named Zoyenka accused me of stealing change from an empty jar of bleach we kept for donations to the Red Cross. The jar of bleach in question never had more than a total of eighty cents, mostly in pennies and nickels. Of course I hadn't done it—but once I'd asked someone for twenty-five cents out of the jar for the parking garage, and Zoyenka never let me live it down.

"People like you make me sick," Zoyenka said to me. They removed me from office and another girl got put in my place.

Later, I found out that Zoyenka got caught red-handed stealing money from the salon she had worked for. Side-eye emoji, hunny, and snap!

Anywho, I was so relieved to find out that I loved doing hair, and loved working with people, as much as I'd hoped. Even when I got frustrated—like the time I drop-kicked a mannequin's head through a window while I was learning finger waves—I still felt like I was becoming my best self. And after the disaster of Arizona, it felt good to not be a hot mess. For the first time in a while, I felt normal.

I had expected Minnesota to have really gorgeous summers, but that's a full lie: it's, like, 103 degrees there in the summer, with 97 percent humidity. It was the first time I ever saw my cat Bug actually pant during one particular heat wave. We kept thinking it was going to break, but the temperature just kept climbing.

I called my mom, desperate. "My cat's gonna die of dehydration," I said. "I have to get an air conditioner—please put some money in my account."

Begrudgingly, she agreed, and me and my dear friend Tasia went looking for a window AC unit to install in my sweltering apartment. But by the time we'd made it to our seventh Home Depot, it started to dawn on us that every air conditioner within fifty miles was sold out. I called my mom, crying, in a panic.

She found a sporting goods store that sold air conditioners in Duluth, over two hours away, so we drove there to pick it up. When we brought it home, I went into my bedroom to retrieve the little box of tools we'd need to install it. While I was in there, I heard something crash in the living room. I ran out to see Tasia—a five-foot-ten, former figure-skating swan of a young woman—bracing herself against a couch. In her heat-stricken desperation, she had kicked the screen out of our second-story window and was now feverishly duct-taping the air conditioner into the window, shoving pieces of couch cushioning, socks, broken-apart Styrofoam cooler bits, and loose papers into the exposed slats on either side of the unit to seal it in.

I looked at her. "Holy shit, Tasia! The window!"

"Jonathan!" she yelped. "Your cat is panting! I'm freaking out!"

I tried to help her. Waterfalls of sweat were burning my eyeballs. Once I felt them stinging my eyes, I realized that Tasia was right. We just had to make it work.

And you know what? It did work. Whenever people asked what unit I was in in my apartment building, I'd just tell them it was the one with the air conditioner secured on either side by mounds of broken Styrofoam bits, magazines, throw pillows, and duct tape. Was it an eyesore? Yes. Was it effective? Kind of. A few feet around the window was markedly cooler than the rest of the hot-yoga-temperature apartment. Mission accomplished.

* * *

I loved my time in Minneapolis, but I knew I couldn't live there. They had a very oversaturated market for hairdressers because of all the hair schools there. Also, it was really cold in the winters, and obviously summers were horrendous. I was ready for a different kind of *heat*, honey.

On our midterm weeklong vacation from hair school, I traveled to Phoenix, since my dad's parents lived there a few months out of the year, and I'd thought it would be a good place to live and do hair after graduation. I wanted to get to know my paternal grandmother, who had been diagnosed with this really, really bad ovarian cancer when I was in third grade that had spread all over her body. Her liver, lungs, everywhere. She was told to get her affairs in order because there was no treatment available for the terminal nature of her cancer. She smiled and asked for a second opinion, and the second opinion wasn't different. So she smiled and got a third, and they said they would treat her. She may have lost her hair and lost her hearing but she beat the shit out of that cancer and defied all the odds. She showed me from a young age what grit and determination look like when you are the only one who believes in yourself. That was some badass energy I needed to get to know better, in addition to the fact that I was afraid I would turn into a colossal methball if I moved to a big city like New York or Los Angeles.

One salon in particular that I interviewed at really stood out. So after I graduated, I moved to Scottsdale, where I got a job working there—Salon Beatrix Kiddo. Scottsdale was the capital of fake blondes, fake boobs, and $20,000 "millionaires"—who were driving whatever the equivalent of a Tesla was in 2006, but were actually completely upside down on their mortgage and endlessly in debt. It seemed that everyone was heterosexual and had questionable attitudes, but I was just so happy to be working and doing hair.

My career as a hairdresser was unfolding gorgeously, but being part of a group like in swim team or cheerleading gave me a social circle and something I looked forward to. Now in Phoenix, for the first time in a long time, I didn't have an activity to keep me busy outside of work, and it had me feeling wayward. I then got head-over-heels infatuated with a boy named Viktor Baryshnikov who danced for the Phoenix Ballet Company, and it felt like he was constantly reflecting my own not-enoughness back to me: Like, if you're this gorgeous sick ballet dancer and I'm kinda chunky and don't do anything, what does that mean? I found myself regaling him with tales from my cheerleading days in every millisecond of silence that fell between us, which must have been annoying because it even annoyed me saying it. But his gorgeousness and talent left me feeling bleak and meager. He ghosted me on a Christmas text, and I had to drive past his apartment building on the way to work every day, which killed me. It also made Kelly Clarkson's *My December* hit me like a ton of bricks. The bridge on "Sober"? Turn on the windshield wipers!

But it was also a period where I grew a lot and learned that I could show up for myself—and the people around me. My grandma lived in north Scottsdale, a forty-five-minute drive from the salon, and I'd promised that I would keep her looking fresh. So every Friday I would leave my house, drive forty-five minutes to her house, pick her up, drive her forty-five minutes back to the salon, wash her hair, blow-dry it, and then drive her another forty-five minutes home. At the salon, she insisted on going around to every single old lady there and saying to them, in a totally endearing but slightly condescending way, "Hi, Susan—so good to see you! You look so beautiful today!" It was her way of saying, "Wow, you old bag, good for you for coming out and getting your crusty mop washed." She was so spunky—it was like she didn't realize that she was approximately the same age as them. It was the first time I could remember really keeping a commitment to someone else, and it showed me that I could actually kind of be a grown-up.

Back then, a typical blow-dry cost $35. But my dad's mom was a child of the Depression, so she would, very generously, break me off a hot $8.50—counting out a five-dollar bill, three ones, and two quarters as payment for the four hours it took me to drive her around and do her hair. She thought she was the best tipper, and I could never tell her otherwise. I was basically paying to do her hair. Eventually my dad called my grandpa and was, like, "Dad, the kid's making $18,000 a year—can you please have her pay him something?" She was tighter than the bark on a tree, as my mom would say.

Through three years of having the privilege of that weekly

blow-dry time with Noonie, as I called her, a larger growing forgetfulness led to an increasingly problematic diagnosis—dementia. (You really can't tell if it's Alzheimer's for sure until the person is deceased.) My grandfather—who was a doctor who served in the Korean War and had remained fiercely independent—was determined to take care of her and didn't want her to go into a home. I think he felt extraordinarily devoted to protecting her because of how she had cared for him when, six years prior, he'd been the victim of a freak accident. My grandma had lost her balance getting off the toilet in the middle of the night and when she called for him, he reached down to turn off the water to the toilet and the tank fell and severed part of his hand. He nearly died, but because he was a doctor he was as cool as a cucumber. When they sewed his hand back together, it was barely usable. As my grandmother's mental health deteriorated, she thought he was a weird pterodactyl who had kidnapped her. She constantly thought her parents were about to come home. They had been dead for, like, sixty years.

She ultimately wound up being hospitalized and her condition worsened rapidly. My uncle came to help us get her from the hospital back to her hometown of Bloomington, Illinois. It seemed weird for this to happen in their vacation home, and it was really important to the family to get her back home alive. Noonie was always endlessly chic, but as they were readying her to go to the airport, they had dressed her in a dowdy-ass wind-breaker.

"She is not going to wear that on the plane," I said.

Even if her mind was rapidly losing itself, I knew she would never wear that outside.

"It's fine," my uncle said. "Trust me."

No less than ten minutes later, I heard her screaming from the bedroom.

"Kermerlin, I'm not wearing that, I WON'T WEAR IT."

Some gentle frustrated groans and tussling ensued when I went in and calmly pulled out a gorgeous little navy-blue Salvatore Ferragamo vest for her, with cute little slacks and saddle shoes, and got her ready to go on the plane.

Back in Bloomington, she settled into a home, which my grandfather had begrudgingly agreed to place her in for end-of-life care. The doctors had said that while her brain was deteriorating her body was still very strong, so they thought she would be there for a while. That stressed out my family, wondering if they would have the money to cover a long-term, high-level-of-care stay. But my grandma had defied the odds before and I believe she was in control of her body still. Because being the insanely cheap and thoughtful woman she was, her condition ended up deteriorating more quickly than anyone expected. Within only a couple weeks, she was gone. That was simply money she wasn't going to spend. Saving her family the anguish of watching their loved one slide away slowly over years, I believe she made the choice to go when she did. She died on my twenty-second birthday.

It was the first time I had needed to step up to the plate as an adult in my dad's family. I'd been so helpful with her in the last years of her life that my grandfather let me move into his house in Scottsdale, where I lived for several months, rent-free, while I saved money and tried to build my independence. When she first died, I was acutely aware that for the rest of my life, my birthday would be the day she had died. But then I realized how incredible it was that she had chosen the day I came into the world as the day for her to start her new journey out of this world, on to her next adventure. Thank you for being fearless, Noonie, and Ma. My two beautiful grandmas who I wouldn't be myself without and who I miss every single day.

I found other ways to grow too. My friend Anatolia, who was my station partner at the salon, introduced me to Bikram yoga, which started my journey of actually becoming healthy for the first time. In the beginning, I would smoke five Parliament Light 100s on my way to yoga, and usually leave in the middle to take a smoke break, which Bikram yoga really frowns upon—they advise you staying in the hot room at all costs. Puke, poop, pee? Deal with it! Stay in the room.

After doing Bikram literally every day for an entire year, I discovered Vinyasa Flow, and pretty soon I had transitioned from hot yoga to a much floatier practice. Yoga at that time for me was all about ego—how long could I do a handstand, can I get into these splits, oh my God I wonder if that guy thinks I'm hot?—but then over time my connection to spirituality deepened. I read *The Four Agreements*, and *The Power of Now*, and *A New Earth*, and everything Deepak Chopra ever wrote. The Bhagavad Gita. The Upanishads. The story of Siddhartha. And, honey, I read *Skinny Bitch* and that book traumatized me so deeply I became a militant vegan for four years

With the internal came the external. I really built my client base as a hairdresser in Scottsdale. Within nine months, I was booked and busy. There was lots of good feedback and lots of good word-of-mouth buzz. Even my family was proud of me. For the first time, I didn't need help with my rent.

In Phoenix, people typically made their money in the winter before all the snowbirds left for the summer. But in the summer of 2008, the economy dropped the fuck out. Five of my clients committed suicide. When I came to work on a Tuesday morning, my books would be full. By the afternoon, half my clients would have canceled. By the next morning, another 20 percent would have canceled. I'd have to go out onto the street and beg people: "I'll do your haircut for $30 and your highlights for free if you come in right now."

The Great Recession hit Phoenix hard. And after a few months of that, I knew I had to get out. I wanted to go to Los

Angeles—both because I knew business would be better there and also because I genuinely wanted to become a better hair-stylist. With my grandmother no longer needing my help in Phoenix, and knowing that I had been responsible enough to show up for her when she needed me, I felt like I had my green light. Besides, in Phoenix, no matter how I foiled someone's hair, everything looked like Kelly Clarkson–circa 2002 in a bad way—chunky, piano-key highlights. In LA, people were bring-ing a more lived-in style of color, and I didn't know how to cre-ate those looks.

Anatolia and I had heard about a woman in Los Angeles who charged $650 to do your highlights, who had basically in-vented balayage—the art of hand-painted hair. Anatolia wanted to go study under her. And I was ready to follow.

* * *

So off we went to Los Angeles, loading all our stuff and Bug into my car, ready for a new adventure. Anatolia had moved a few months earlier to do the assistant program at Tonia Skoekenkaya Tutberidze, a newly opened, all-the-rage place to be seen and the absolute best place to get your hair done. There was a specific energy about it that was like nothing I'd ever experienced before. Anatolia had started calling me to give me verbal directions on how to do balayage after she got out of class, but I didn't always understand exactly what she meant, so I fucked up some serious hair trying to learn how to hand-paint highlights. I was down to take her advice on what she was learning at Tonia Skoekenkaya Tutberidze, but I knew that kind of environment wasn't for me as I set out looking for a job.

I'd heard about one particular Aveda salon in LA, and I had my heart set on working there. But in the interview, you actually had to assist a hairdresser on the floor, and I fucked mine up badly: I talked the colorist's ear off. I talked the client's ear off. I got her back wet. I was way overeager. I could tell the stylist wasn't into it.

I was devastated. I had identified so much with Aveda and it was so important to me, but I quickly realized it was kind of a midwestern thing, that didn't have as much of a foothold on the coasts. People in LA wanted more luxurious brands. But I didn't know anything about that.

Now I had blown my big LA opportunity, and the little money I had saved up for my move to LA was dwindling fast. Soon I'd be broke.

The weekend after the botched interview, Anatolia called me. "Can you get here right now?" she said. "This boy just showed up to work literally high and disoriented and he can barely speak so he definitely can't work today and they just fired him and now they need someone with a license who can fill in in a pinch today!"

"Oh my God, yes!" I said, and I was off to Tonia Skoeken-kaya Tutberidze.

The bustle was indescribable. You stood up three inches straighter and held your shoulders the fuck back. The assistants were strutting like Naomi Campbell on the floor just to get someone a cup of water.

I was assisting a stylist named Czarina. She looked like a young Supreme—take-your-breath-away gorgeous, with a triangular-shaped fro and smoky lavender Stella McCartney thigh-high boots and skinny jeans and an oversized sweater—the baddest most feroshist. I was enamored.

I was naturally inclined toward formulating color: my eyes understood it, my brain got in lockstep with color theory much easier. The three-dimensionality of a haircut intimidated me. What I knew how to do best was how to curl my long layers so you couldn't see how fucked up the haircuts were.

Even though I had always seen myself as more of a colorist than a stylist, I was still excited to work with Czarina because getting out of my colorist comfort zone was important. Plus in this world of luxury hairstyling you either color or you cut, you don't do both. The boy who I was replacing was a stylist's assistant, so that's the role I stepped into because I was ready to learn everything I could when it came to cutting and styling hair. Plus I knew I would still learn gorgeous sums of color knowledge by working so closely and watching such incredible artists.

When Czarina's first client arrived, I started talking up a storm. "What did you do this morning?" I asked the client. "Oh, me, I got a smoothie and then I went to yoga!"

I didn't realize that my job was to go in and be seen and not heard. For someone like me who was used to having a clientele of my own and having people give a shit about me, this new role wasn't going to be easy. I was talking up a storm, having so much fun. I wanted Czarina to love me. She was such an incredible hairdresser: She could style Afros to look like they were flat-ironed with just a round brush and a blow-dryer. She had done hair at the Victoria's Secret Fashion Show for years. I wanted to be able to give blow-dries as straight as she could, to set the hair in a way that it could stand up to Hurricane Maria and still look slayed. I wanted to deliver an updo so good that it could make Serge Normant cry. No matter what the client needed to achieve, Czarina could make it happen and never break a sweat.

After my first day assisting her, another senior assistant pulled me aside. "Okay, here's the thing," she said. "You can't talk like you did today—that was insane. These people have known Czarina for years. Nobody cares about the smoothie you had this morning. Your job is to relax them, help her be nice, keep us on time, and stay quiet."

"Got it," I said.

"Next Tuesday," she said, "they'll have you back and you can try out for Natacha."

Czarina was a very busy stylist on her own, but her best friend was Natacha, and the company required one assistant to help with both of them. The following Tuesday morning, at Tonia Skoekenkaya Tutberidze salon, the click-click-click of heels perked up my gay ears. I did a 180-pivot turn to reveal a blunt-fringe wavy-bob and the most gorgeous freckles I've ever seen caressing the face of a hairdressing queen with a cute LBD and the most moisturized legs I've ever seen. To this day, I just want to eat ice cream off her legs. I've never been attracted to a woman, but Natacha just had this sexy swag that made my titties perk. She's the type of hairdresser who could cut the best haircut you've ever seen with both hands tied behind her back using only her teeth because she is just. That. Bitch. Best hairdresser I've ever seen. But if you say that to her, she'll punch you in the face because she doesn't take compliments well.

I was on my best behavior. Somehow, my puppy-dog energy was just cute enough and just not annoying enough that it worked out. And I was hired.

Tonia Skoekenkaya Tutberidze was the place to be, for anyone who was everyone. It was so bustling and so sought-after. I went from being someone who charged $50 to give a haircut to assisting people who charged $200 for a haircut—it was a whole different playing field.

I loved being there. I quickly met all these other assistants who were working hard, which meant there was this gorgeous community of assistants together, who all hung out after work.

But it was also incredibly fast-paced. The women I assisted were working quickly. They could do seven or eight clients a day, which meant I was blow-drying fourteen to eighteen heads per shift. They would do the front, and I would do the back, and you had to do it on the same speed and timing they did, but also not talk or ask questions in the middle of anything, plus you had to be checking in the new clients and checking out the old ones, and also if a client was getting their color done with another colorist after their cut you had to be responsible, as the assistant, for getting them to the colorist on time. It was so many moving parts, and if anything went wrong, which inevitably happened with hair color because it's time-consuming and fraught with unseen pitfalls, not to mention difficult, it was always the assistant's fault. We were paid minimum wage and had to work crazy hours, and you could never forget that this was not about you. They didn't just make you feel that way, they would tell you to your face. The message was: Get used to it, and get back to work.

From my perspective, the manager of that salon was drunk with power. She kept a stack of assistants' résumés on her desk at all times just to keep us on our toes, not to mention most people couldn't last more than three months so she needed them at the ready. I was one of the ones she was nice to, because she liked my personality and that I was quick, but I never got too comfortable because on the inside I knew she was cold as ice.

And all the famous people! A celebrity who shall remain nameless—she's a D-lister, anyway—would bring an entourage of six people while she was getting her hair done at Tonia Skoekenkaya Tutberidze, then call the paparazzi on herself so they'd get a picture of her new lewk as she was leaving.

Meanwhile, I'd see an icon like Jane Fonda come in for a blow-dry, polished, kind, and the epitome of class. That's the kind of fiercedom I could get behind. I even got to work with her hairstylist a few times and got to wash her hair.

After one of those times, she complimented my long hair and said, "It makes you look like Jesus." I felt so seen I could barely even go about my day.

Years later, right after *Queer Eye* was announced, Netflix invited the Fab Five to the *Grace and Frankie* premiere. Jane was there with Lisa Kudrow and Lily Tomlin. I wanted to introduce myself, but my show wasn't out yet—what right did I have to go talk to Jane Fonda?

Bobby was ballsier than I was. He walked right over and introduced us. She tolerated us, very politely. Then suddenly the words were bursting out of my mouth. "Jane," I said, "I'm so sorry to do this I just love you so much and you used to call me

Jesus at Tonia Skoekenkaya Tutberidze when I was the fill-in assistant and I used to wash your hair and I love *Grace and Frankie* so much and I'm just so excited to be here."

She got a little twinkle in her eye. "I remember you."

"That was me!"

I curtsied and we shook hands. We exchanged congratulations, and I nearly sharted.

I've never gotten over the Jane Fonda of it all. Every so often, I think about the fact that my picture is next to her on the same platform and it totally blows my mind.

The great televangelist Joyce Meyer once said: "Don't put God in a box." And it's true—you never know where you're gonna end up.

* * *

Anatolia and I would drive back to Scottsdale to do our clients there every other weekend, which took a toll on us. After working sixty-hour weeks for eight dollars an hour, we would drive Saturday, from 6 p.m. until 1 a.m., then we would do twelve clients each on Sunday and then eight-ish clients on Monday, all with no assistants, then drive back to Los Angeles on Monday night, arriving at 1 a.m. or later so I could be back at work at 8 a.m. on Tuesday at Tonia Skoekenkaya Tutberidze, then work until Saturday again. I did that sort of schedule for years, and it ran me ragged. But that's what we had to do to make ends meet.

In the service industry if you don't go to work and do work, you don't eat.

But I loved my clients. I loved getting to check in on them. At Tonia Skoekenkaya Tutberidze, I saw colorists who charged $750 just to touch a highlight on your head. They were masters at balayage, whereas I had only ever foiled hair. I was witnessing beautiful transformations from the most talented colorists in the industry, right in front of my face. And at the salon, you had to be willing to be an assistant for a really long time before they would let you into that club.

Part of moving to Los Angeles was learning to perfect my craft. I was really driven to be successful and actually good at doing hair. Part of that was financial, but it was also because I've always had an indescribable drive to be good—to have an invite to the party. Truthfully, I'm so competitive that I'll let it run me into the ground: maybe not to the point where I'll hurt myself, but I'll lose sleep over it. If I'm passionate about something, I won't give up on it until I master it. (If I don't care about something, it's like pulling teeth to get me to even attempt it in the first place.)

Leaving work, I would cry on the drive home and continue crying as I was making myself dinner. I was so scared that I would never wrap my head around the three-dimensional nature of hair. I kept seeing Natacha do it right, but when it came to my haircut—it just didn't look like that.

Every Thursday, we took class with one particular educator

named Mikhail—someone who always rode inappropriateness to a razor's edge. He was always there with a gross joke nobody wanted to hear, but with a heart of gold...ish.

As an assistant, if your boss finished early but you hadn't hit your overtime yet, they would keep you on to work with someone else. Once they kept me on to work with a stylist who had a scary reputation that I'd never worked with before.

On certain days he'd be great and fun to work for, but on other days, he would make you cry for the sport of it. All the top stylists were very particular about blow-drying and styling from the ears forward, while you did it from the ears backward, so one boss would be doing the front left side, while you'd be doing the back right side, which meant you were never on the same side of the head.

On this day, after I'd been at Tonia's for eight months, Ygor needed me to do the back of a woman's blow-dry. At that point, I only knew how to use metal brushes, as opposed to bristle brushes, which he was using. I was doing it the best I could but it was flipping out—it wasn't lying totally straight.

When I finished the back of her hair, he looked at it.

"I asked you to make this straight," he said.

"Ygor, I'm sorry," I said. "I don't know how to do it with a boar bristle brush."

"No, faggot, I want you to get it straight with the brush I asked you to use," he said, leaning in to my ear. He took the brush out of my hand and threw it to the floor. "I hope you die of AIDS," he said. "Get away from me."

When I told the manager what had happened, she shrugged it off. "Yeah," she said. "Ygor can get pretty intense sometimes, but he never says no to a client. That's why we like him." This sort of aggressive behavior was commonplace in the salon and something I thought was necessary to endure to reach my goals as a bad bitch hairdresser.

To get onto the floor, we had to do ten "checkoffs"—certain haircuts that we had to execute well. I had to do ten just right in order to pass as a stylist able to take new clients from the front desk.

Mikhail was a high-level educator at the salon, and both he and your boss had to be in the salon with no clients booked in order to watch you do the haircut and check it off to pass you. Getting both of those extremely busy people to be at the salon at the same day at the same time—especially when Mikhail was only there three days a week—was next to impossible.

But I found a model who was willing to let me try a shag so I could get that checkoff in the bag. It was cheer tryouts on hair level stress: while you're doing the haircut, they're watching you, and you can feel your heart in between your eyeballs as they watch every cut you make, but you have to seem very in control—and you can't just be quiet and focus, you have to be good on the floor, and conversational, and charming.

So I did what, to me, looked like the most modern fabulous shag. Mikhail preferred shags like Lisa Rinna's hair, that look like you've been electrocuted—really big, really piecey, really textured. That's not my aesthetic—even if it was the salon's aesthetic—so I was just trying to create a shag shape that wouldn't make the client want to Yelp my ass into oblivion. Not a voluminous Lisa Rinna shag—a flatter, more *L Word* shag.

Natacha checked the haircut and said it was perfect. But when Mikhail checked it, he said even though it was technically perfect, they couldn't check me off on it because it was too flat on top. (It wasn't flat, it just wasn't 1987-electrocution style.)

I was so crushed. I went down to the alley and stifled back tears before returning to assist for Natacha that afternoon.

Mikhail was a savage. In classes, he would rip the scissors from my hands. "Can you explain to me why you're lost in this haircut and actively fucking it up and not asking for help?" he'd say. "Can you explain why this section is completely incorrect and you're completely perpendicular when I'm telling you to be parallel?" The model would be sitting, frozen, in the chair. "Why are you actively fucking up this haircut?"

One week we were learning a rock 'n' roll shag technique, inspired by Ashlee Simpson: chin-length face-framing, but then collarbone in the back, like a long fashion-y mullet with lots of face-framing to make it really wispy.

I had one client, Nicola, whose hair I'd been cutting back in Scottsdale for years, who had also moved to Los Angeles around the time I did. Typically, I did her hair at midnight at my house after I got off my shifts, because I had also brought the first salon chair I'd ever had from Arizona to Los Angeles in order to do clients at my house.

We had very strict monthly education classes where we would have to provide a model for specific haircuts. If your model canceled last minute, or was a no-show, you would find yourself begging strangers on the street, in a coffee shop, or at the mall in the forty-five minutes after work before the class to find your replacement. During Ashlee Simpson week, a model canceled on me, so I called Nicola and asked if she would sit for me.

She said she was down to try the new haircut, but she needed to preserve her length, which the supervisor said would be fine.

I had just finished cutting the first section of her hair when Mikhail came over. "Jonathan," he said, "that guide length is way too long."

"I know, Mikhail," I said. "But you said we could do it halfway down her neck, instead of chin length."

"No," he said, irritated, "I said the top of the lip."

He took the scissors from my hands, took the entire side of her hair, and cut it off to her top lip—cutting a full eight inches from the length of her hair. Then he put the scissors down and walked away.

Nicola looked at me, stunned. Horrified. "Jonathan," she said. "One second."

She jumped off the chair, pulled two minibottles of vodka from her bag, and chugged them, one after another, then turned to me. "Keep going," she said.

"Nicola," I said, panicking, "if I make the back longer, it's going to be a full mullet. It won't be a fashion mullet. It's going to be a literal mullet."

"Just do what you need to do."

"I can do a tiny little lip bob," I said. "Or a Dutch pageboy! Or a true mullet. What do you want?"

"The bob!" she said. "The bob! Just do the bob!"

It was supposed to be a shag, but it ended up looking like a helmet. By the end we were both ugly-crying like we were at a funeral.

"What are you doing?" Mikhail said when he finally saw it finished. "That's not anywhere near a shag!"

Nicola got so drunk that night she had to come sleep at my apartment. In bed, tossing and turning, I thought about how she would never come back to me.

But Nicola still followed me to every salon I ever went to. Those types of people, who were that fiercely loyal—they made it all worthwhile.

Growth often happens when we're uncomfortable. During those years, processing my personal experiences and professional experiences provided for so much growth because I spent so much time in discomfort having to learn and be quick on my feet.

I wanted to get on the floor at Tonia Skoekenkaya Tutberidze with every last fiber of my being. But after nearly two years, still working as an assistant and having the goalposts for what I'd need to become a stylist constantly moving, I knew that I wasn't going to make it there. It wasn't worth giving up my well-being and working in a toxic and frequently abusive environment to make 20 percent from a clientele that I knew I would have to build myself. (You read that right—once you got on the floor and got to start charging $200 for haircuts you only got to pocket $40 plus the tip.) For that time of learning and exposure to a different level of excellence, I was grateful. But now I was armed with the knowledge of the kind of boss I wanted to grow into, the kind of person I wanted to be, and I had more importantly learned the worth of saying "This isn't worth it."

When I finally quit to go work at another salon, I was devastated. But unlike when I'd left college, I didn't feel like a failure. I knew something better was coming.

CHAPTER 8

MR. CLEAN

REMEMBER EVERYTHING ABOUT THE NIGHT I MET SERGEI.

It was November 22, 2010, and I was out in West Holly-wood. It had been a long day at Tonia Skoekenkaya Tut-beridze, and like any hardworking, red-blooded American, I was ready to let my hair down. Back when I was living in Tucson, I'd met this boy named Alyosha—a really cute biracial boy who wore a full face of MAC makeup everywhere he went. We'd met at my first gay party when I was cheering at the University of Arizona, where I was a seventeen-year-old college freshman, and he was still a senior in high school. He'd come hang out at my apartment, show me around town, and introduce me to the Tucson gays.

Alyosha was a sweetheart, but he was extremely traum due to a very vuln past that rendered him mildly alcoholic adjacent—he had a nasty habit of drunk driving. But he was right in my friend arousal template and I attracted those kinds of people with my bleeding heart. I love someone with a story—always have, always will. So I wasn't surprised when I got a call from a WeHo gay bar called Trunks that Alyosha was blackout drunk and lain out on the bar, and if someone didn't come to pick him up, they were going to call the police.

When I got to Trunks, there Alyosha was, facedown on the bar. But standing against the wall, there was another guy I'd never seen before. He was like a bald black Mr. Clean: six foot three and striking, with big brown venti mocha latte eyes and a big ol' muscular chest. His name was Sergei. And he was alone.

"Is anyone sitting here?" I said, pointing to the seat next to him at the bar. He shook his head no. So I picked Alyosha up like a sack of potatoes, threw him over my shoulder, put him in my car, locked the door, and went back into the bar.

"I'm meeting friends at the Abbey," he said. "Do you want to join us?"

"Sure," I said. "I'd love to." We called Anatolia to come pick up Alyosha and off we went. I could only hear every third word he was saying, because the music was deafening, but it didn't matter. All that mattered was that he wanted to hold my hand and I was instantly in love.

Sergei and I went to every bar in West Hollywood that night. Our conversations weren't deep, but they were playful. I couldn't believe that a boy taller than I was, with a toothy grin, who was visually so masc-for-masc could be into a hippie vegan topknot yogi like me.

When he dropped me off at home, we made out—but we didn't hook up. That was unusual for me because typically I would have had him park his car, come up to my place, and vanish into the wind, never to be seen nor heard from again. But not this time. There was something wholesome about Sergei. I really liked him. I could see my stepdad walking me down the aisle of St. John's Episcopal already.

Two days later, the next time we hung out, we watched TV and ordered in vegan food. I was proud of myself for making it to the second night before we hooked up. It was the first time I could remember that I felt really connected with a guy I was having sex with. I felt validated in my humanity instead of a degraded mess. My mom had always told me as a teenager that sex was meant to be two spirits coming together. Taking someone inside you is allowing their spirit inside you. Ew, Mom! Gross! But she really did tell me that, and as I experienced connected sex for the first time, I was both riled that the speech she gave me as a teenager was rattling around in my brain and also vaguely comforted that she had turned out to be right.

On our first real date, Sergei picked me up and took me to the Getty in his car.

That day at the Getty was so gorgeous and magical. It was my first time there, and I couldn't believe how shocking it all was—all that white marble. He held my hand. He wasn't afraid to hold my hand. We took cute pictures positioned like we were at prom—him standing behind me. There was no piece of him that felt ashamed about those moments of public affection, and that meant something to me. He was the first person I didn't see as being remotely ashamed of me.

One of my early boyfriends once put his arm around me leaving school, and the instant shame caused me to recoil. So often for gay people, sex and attraction is kept behind closed doors. Of the numerous people I'd been with sexually, there were maybe two total I would've felt good about being seen with. Sergei was the ideal image of a partner, the manifestation of every dream I never knew I had.

I also loved how I felt when people looked at us. I loved how we looked together. I've noticed that a lot of people in the LGBTQ+ fam—specifically the L and G—have a tendency to date our identical twins or polar opposites, which I think is just so cute. This isn't a blanket statement—just a gentle observache. With Sergei I could feel the balancing of each other, his masculine to my feminine. He was the captain of the football team and I was the head cheerleader.

Once I met Sergei, the mixture of oxytocin, endorphins, vasopressin, testosterone, and estrogen was so intense and exacting that I'm still not sure I'm over it or ever will be fully. He was my first true love.

I flexed my butt cheeks every time he grabbed my butt for the first four months. I was so busy trying to be what I thought he wanted, which, for some reason, I was sure was nothing more than a really tight butt.

We had a fundamental disconnect in how we communicated our needs, especially in terms of how we communicated in bed. The way we connected sexually didn't match the level of intensity I had experienced through so many years of casual app-driven or under-the-influence sexual behavior. (After all, I'd been a very busy girl.) I was unable to tell him what I wanted and needed, which was a great level of intimacy. But we had differences in how we did our gorgeous horizontal tango. Falling in love in what felt like my first real adult relationship and not having him seem to want to passionately throw me around the way I thought he would hurt. And being young, gay, and new to how our gorgeous butts work during sexy-time put strain on our relationship. Because I didn't feel that fire from Sergei, it set me up to feel rejected.

Moreover: I didn't have much time with him. He was such a hard worker. And he had created a good life for himself through nothing but hard work—nobody had helped him. He worked overnight—from 11 p.m. to 5 a.m.—and then would go to a coffee shop, where he worked as a manager. Then he would sleep from 4 p.m. until 10:30 p.m., then go back to work.

So pretty soon I found myself in a relationship with someone who had thirty minutes a day to give. He was so exhausted all the time that by Sundays, he was a zombie. And that wasn't going to change anytime soon.

My mom was a work addict, and even though of course I knew how much she loved me, if your love language is quality time and you're not getting that, it doesn't matter how much someone tells you they love you—you need the quality time. (If I lost you at "love language," put this book down and read *The 5 Love Languages*, because that shit is major. Actually, don't put this book down—just google it really quick, then read it after you're done with this book.) Looking back on it, it's interesting that the first person I fell in love with was similar to my mom in that way. They could show me with their actions and tell me with their words that they loved me, but they couldn't make the time if I lit myself on fire. So, to answer your question, yes: I fell in love with a big black muscular version of my mom.

I didn't always like us together. I always wanted what he didn't have to give me. And for my part, I couldn't accept him for who he was, and where he was.

But, honey, the beginning was gorgeous. Getting tipsy on Sunday Funday, him coming to my house from work the night before to crawl into bed when he didn't have to work at the coffee shop.

The first time he ever came with me to yoga, I was nervous because I wore tights with shorts over them to practice in. We were sitting on the couch, and I was in my underwear, and I stood up to get ready. Then I turned to face him.

"I have to tell you something," I said. "I wear tights to yoga. American Apparel tights and a low-cut, droopy racer-back tank. Serving major Richard Simmons realness."

He looked at me funny. "Okay," he said. "I wear basketball shorts. Is that okay?"

"Yeah," I said. "But I'm going to wear tights."

"Okay," he said. "That's great. And can you stop flexing your butt every time I grab it, babe?"

I was so scared that he was going to reject me. But it didn't even dawn on him that my tights might make me seem feminine, or that people might judge us. At the time I was still trying to masc it up. Even on Grindr, pre-Sergei, I would very much be like, "Sup, bro?" (Or possibly the ultracasual and even more simple "Sup?") Even telling that story now, I feel waves of shame because while I've become confident and I now love my feminine side, growing to love that part of me took a long time. Now all I can do is shower that wounded part of myself that rejected their femininity with compassion and be grateful that I shook off the shackles of toxic masculinity.

Sergei accepted me as I was. I loved that about him—that he thought I was cute no matter how I dressed, that he didn't think I was too femme. Of course, he worked every night and every day and would only have a few hours a week for me. But at that point, I was so relieved to find someone who would accept me and love me at all, even if they could only give me a few crumbs of their cake, that it felt like enough.

Until it didn't.

Before moving to LA, I would cruise on gay.com and later Grindr, when that first came out. As life and work got more intense, my hookups did too—in ways that were risky, and soul-eroding. I'd find myself in an impenetrable bubble of searching for something—usually a much older man who was into role-playing the same scenarios that happened to me as a kid. I was trying to re-create these events from my childhood, only in this version, I was the one who had control. I didn't have the language to explain what this acting-out was about, but through tons of therapy I've learned that this was my trauma's way of working its way out when I reached my threshold for tolerating everything from my unprocessed past, my job, and my relationship with Sergei. As my pain points were triggered, this was how I self-medicated. I felt driven to have hookups like this by some out-of-this-world part of me that was fixated on re-creating these situations to give *me* this sense of power, because now I could choose where, when, and how my space was entered. I always used condoms—I was terrified of getting STDs—but I had this way of finding myself back in the bubble.

The first couple times this happened, it felt extremely scary. The mixture of adrenaline and endorphins and panic and excitement was very similar to what I had felt as a kid. What I wasn't prepared for was the cycle that that created. After I'd been retraumatized, in the days that followed, I was overcome with a sense of shame and grief and panic. What kind of person does this? Who wants to do this? I wasn't even on drugs. What did it mean if this was something I craved? The shame ran down into a fundamental belief of what I was worth. Which wasn't a lot. I didn't know how to deal with it. As I bottled up the shame, it would build and build until I had poked the bear and then I'd be right back in the bubble, looking for it again.

Right before I met Sergei, it had started to feel like an issue—not like it was approaching crisis levels, but I found myself cruising for sex daily as opposed to weekly. I chalked it up to being in a new city with a ton of gay people around. After all, if you've been on the Atkins diet for twenty-one years and then all of a sudden you find yourself in the middle of the Girl Scout bakery, or Taco Bell headquarters, what do you think is going to happen? I think everyone has the propensity for compulsivity in different areas of their life if the factors all align.

Back in Arizona, I had been on the floor as a hairdresser, building my own clientele. When you're in that role, it's almost like you're the star of the show—clients ask you about yourself, and you develop real relationships with people. But in this new job, as an assistant, it was never about me. Everything that went wrong was my fault. No one was shy about letting me know that. The need for validation and the desire to be nurtured and sought after was stronger all of a sudden, because I never felt like I was doing a good job or being seen in any way. Being a survivor of sexual abuse, looking to sex for validation and nurturing felt very normal and comforting to me.

I had been looking to those random hookups over the previous year to fill those gaps in my schedule and in my heart. Once I was with Sergei, I had all this alone time. I didn't have a ton of friends and I had to be bright-eyed and bushy-tailed in the mornings.

So after we'd been together for a few months, I went back on Grindr. It was easy to justify: I thought I could just make friends. I wasn't going to do anything. Maybe we'd trade some dick pics. It was fine. Nothing was going to happen. I knew it was wrong. I knew it was a secret I had to keep. But knowing that something felt wrong, and that I had to keep a secret, was a kind of double life that I was very familiar keeping. When you're a survivor of abuse, living in chaos can be the most upsetting yet comforting thing in the world. It was for me.

As all my epic, face-plant run-me-over-with-your-car moments always have, it started this way: *It's going to be fine. I won't tell anyone. Nothing bad is going to happen.*

Part of me wondered if maybe I needed a therapist who I could talk to about this, because I was starting to get worried about the real-world implications that this behavior could bring to my life. Was it normal that with this handsome drink of water slumbering in bed next to me, all I really wanted was to find an uncle daddy to pretend to play Doctor with me while I was sleeping? Was I a horrible person? Was I incapable of being in a healthy relationship? If I have this propensity to lie to such a good man, do I just fucking suck as a human being? I felt like a prisoner in my mind, as the shame built and built.

I did end up finding a therapist with the help of Natacha, who had morphed into something like a West Coast mom for me. I was hoping to soothe some of those fears, calm down the acting-out behavior, and save my relationship. But the hard thing about therapy is: if you're lying through your teeth through a lil friend of mine I like to call "omission," the therapist can't really do their job. And then you're just clearing out your mom of her hard-earned money for your $160-a-session therapy. God, Mom, I'm sorry for being a shit, but at least I eventually paid off your mortgage, right?

Finally, after several months of mismanaging myself, the dam broke. I cheated on Sergei. It wasn't even with a guy who I could fulfill my shameful fantasies with—he wasn't even someone I was attracted to. It was a means to an end, so I could be done with the constant state of anxiety I felt about the never-ending shame pie I was shoving down my throat every night. I wanted to be in love, but I wanted to be out of pain more.

The day after, Sergei came over after his shift. The secret I'd been so sure I could keep immediately clawed its way out of my throat into his ears upon his arrival. He broke up with me on the spot and left for his night shift.

I spent the next five nights going to the bathhouse and doing things I would later regret—the kind of sex I couldn't have with Sergei. I didn't take any drugs. I didn't need them—I was high on grief. I was just so ravaged emotionally that I had to ravage my body too.

After Bath House Bender-gate, I knew I had to do something. I was at my bottom du jour and I was tired of running from the demons. My therapist had already told me that she thought I was dealing with sexual compulsivity, so I'd started attending a twelve-step group for sex addiction in West Hollywood, which was a lot of beautifully damaged queens, just like me, who gave me a real look at recovery, but also the kinds of consequences I might face if I didn't take this seriously. Having Steve's positive experience with a twelve-step program guiding me, I had no qualms about engaging in a recovery of my own. Just like wearing tights in yoga, this was something that I had been nervous to share with Sergei when we were still together, but I did, and he accepted me anyway. He knew that this was something I struggled with, and he'd been supportive—up to the point that I had actually cheated on him.

So with the help of my therapist, to whom I had already fully come clean, I decided to go to an inpatient rehab in Tennessee that had a sex addiction unit. I called Sergei the night before I went, and he came over, and I told him about my week in the bathhouse, and we both cried.

"Can we talk while I'm there?" I asked him, through choked tears. I really wanted to show him that I didn't want it to be over.

"We'll see, Jackie," he said.

Because of the privilege that my family benefited from financially, and the extreme maternal shame that my mother felt from seeing me struggle so mightily for all those years of abuse and bullying in Quincy, I knew she felt personally responsible for so much of my situation. When I told her I needed help, she was even more desperate than I was for me to get it. She shouldered the financial burden of sending me to rehab. She would have given anything for me to be well. As the old adage says, you're only as happy as your most miserable child.

There was another person she was desperate to see heal. Steve had recently been diagnosed with early-stage bladder cancer. Mom and Steve knew the struggles I had been facing and, as I was going off to rehab, were realizing that the diagnosis he had been given was in actuality not correct. It wasn't early-stage. It was terminal cancer that had spread to his kidneys and liver. He was told he had eleven months to live. But I knew Steve wasn't a quitter.

My mom and Steve had done their best to shelter me from the diagnosis in the first place. When Steve got diagnosed with cancer, he and my mom knew he would beat it. In my family, we used my grandma's miraculous beating of cancer as a benchmark for the power of a positive attitude. Steve had that positivity down, in spades. He had beaten addiction—he would beat cancer too. He had always been one of the most positive people I'd ever met. So this cancer diagnosis, coupled with my mom's wanting to see me get better, had her shielding me from the scope of the day-in and day-out of his exploratory treatment, which kept me from knowing how sick he really was. I was also half a country away, working seven days a week in two states. I couldn't see it with my own eyes.

As he started chemo and began to fight the cancer, my mom didn't hide the severity of it anymore. I started to hear in Steve's voice during our phone calls what pain he was in, and learn about the invasiveness of the treatments. Think bruised peehole. Think tons of blood work. Think endless days of relentless tests. Steve was never a complainer, but he was bruised and battered. I was scared for him. What would happen if my mom had to live without the love of her life?

Through my childhood, I had railed against Steve as a father figure. My mom was my best friend, and when he came along, he changed that dynamic. Suddenly, she was my mom. I resented him for this until I was about eleven years old, when it hit me that I only had seven more years in that house, whereas my mom had the rest of her life to lead. I wouldn't be spending that time in Quincy. She deserved to be happy.

But Steve was an incredible stepdad. He didn't have to love me the way he did, and his willingness to do so made me love him back. In addition to diving backward, he had taught me to change tires, bait a hook, and to drive. He would drive me on the back of his motorcycle while shouting "bad to the bone." He would drive me around extra so we could finish scream-singing "His Eye Is on the Sparrow" from *Sister Act 2*, and you couldn't even afford to get us started on the *Moulin Rouge!* or *Les Misérables* soundtracks. What would happen if I lost him? Who would be there for my mom? Who would be her best friend? I sang Celine Dion's "Because You Loved Me" at their wedding. (Very badly, obv.) But he was my mom's eyes when she couldn't see. He did see the best in her, and I knew it. She didn't deserve to see him fight for his life like that.

Cancer will always be a thief, a greedy bitch who steals the dignity from the people closest to you. It's a fate I could not wish on anyone. This fate, this unfairness, this reality was something I would not face—could not face. I would go out into the world and see that cancer drama and I would raise it a sexual compulsivity retraumatizing disaster of equal proportions in my own life. This part, I had control over.

In retrospect, I know that's why I took a slash-and-burn approach through my own life so hard. It was so much easier to create havoc in my life than to have to face what was going on in Quincy. I know it was so unfair to my mom to have to show up for me and Steve at the same time. But I was doing the best I could. Those annoying fucking parts. They always think they know how to help. That's the thing: they really do think they're helping, because it feels good when you're doing it. But really, honey? It's just wreckage city, and everyone is naked and traumatized.

Once I got to rehab, my therapist said I needed to focus on my recovery and since Sergei and I were broken up and I was in the first year of this new life, no new relationships were suggested. Instead I busied myself in rehab, assuming the role of the pageant mom of the group, doing haircuts and plucking eyebrows in the bathroom. (This was strictly not allowed, but in my mind, so was having bad brows. What choice did I have?) I left treatment, having given my lungs their first working break in eight years. I had a new lease on life and I was ready to get that work-life balance poppin'.

A few weeks after I got back to LA, Sergei and I had started seeing each other again. A few weeks after that, we were together again. So immediately I'm following the program guidelines exceptionally well. And I was a faithful kitten. Back with Sergei and back to seeing the same therapist. This time, I was being fully honest. For a good eight months. Which—roll your eyes all you want, I know you think eight months doesn't sound that long—but consider that from the time I met Sergei until the time I went to rehab, it was only about three months. Eight months of good behavior was a demonstration of maturity ferosha that was giving me life.

Then it came time for my salon Christmas party, and Sergei wouldn't take work off to come with me. I was angry, but more than that, I was hurt. I had been trying so hard to become the kind of partner that he deserved, but he hadn't budged an inch in terms of giving me the types of attention that I needed. If we weren't going to have the type of sex that I wanted, at least could he give me the time? But to no avail.

You probably know where this is headed, gorgeous reader. Pretty soon I had started cheating on him again, and this time I was doing it like it was my job. I was double-lifeing the shit out of that man.

He'd leave for work and I'd be, like, "Bye, babe!" and then have a random person come over. We would be complete skanks. Twice in the span of less than forty minutes. When I saw Sergei that night, I'd smile like everything was fine. Again, I know what you're thinking. I'm an absolute snake.

And then I tried meth for the first time. That's hard for me to write. What I really wanted to do in this book was give it a nickname from *Harry Potter*, like Voldemort—because meth is that one thing that I never thought I could, or would, do. Where I grew up I had seen those mugshot pictures of people's faces ruined by the drug. That could never be me. But as it turns out, it could be me, and would be if I didn't get myself to a place where I could learn to quell the demons eating at me. My life was spiraling before my eyes. I'm writing this now because meth has been and continues to be an epidemic in the gay community that we still don't talk about. My life, and the lives of so many others, has been irrevocably changed by the stigma and shame attached to how gay men use meth, and the silence surrounding it.

So here's what happened. I went to the house of a couple I'd met on Grindr and they were smoking from a pipe and they took a hit and then blew it into my mouth. I immediately freaked out in their room. I knew that I had just crossed a line to a whole new *Requiem for a Dream* level that made me super fucking scared. I left their house, went back to my place, and just stared at the wall in my dark room and cried. The next morning, I went to my therapist and told her what had happened. I knew that I had to come fully clean to Sergei and that I had to go back to rehab. It would be my second straight birthday I was spending in inpatient rehabilitation.

One thing I have come to notice in my life is that recovery for me has not been linear. It's more two steps forward, three back, five forward, two back, so I'm always improving but there are setbacks within the improvement. Growing up around so much twelve-step, and seeing so much abstinence preached in rehab and in church, I started to take on an idea that healing had to be all or nothing, which has really not been my truth. A lot of people do hit a rock bottom, find a mode of healing that works, and never mess up again. For me, I was trying to untangle sexual abuse, drug abuse, and PTSD, and it was something that for me wasn't conducive to a never-never-smoking-weed-again approach. Just because we mess up doesn't mean all the lessons we learned are undone. Healing can be imperfect. Somewhere I took on some of the dogma that twelve-step holds true that I don't agree with now. I don't believe once an addict, always an addict. I don't believe addiction is a disease that warrants a life sentence. Twelve-step programs saved my stepdad and they helped save me. Finding groups to be open and honest with is of priceless importance, but if you ever mess up or can't string a couple months together without a slipup you're not ruined. There are a million ways to reach recovery. Don't let anyone tell you you can't find a way that works for you.

Last time I was in rehab, I'd felt like I needed to get far away from my environment, but this time I wanted to stay close to home. I thought that would give me a better shot at integrating after I got out. And Sergei didn't cut me off like a dead foot this time. Instead, he accepted the fact that sexual compulsivity was something that was going to be a more multifaceted problem to deal with, but he told me if I promised to be honest with him about everything that was going on, this was something we could work through together. There was nothing I wouldn't try to save this relationship. I didn't know if I was worth saving, but this relationship, I knew, had to be. There was no choice.

Back in treatment, I saw a vast array of amazing people with different challenges come into that group: heroin addicts, alcoholics, gambling addicts. You name it—we did it. The gooey butter cake they served on Sundays at family day? Legend. The group therapy? Major. I met a girl named Helenskaya who I remain close with to this day. I was happy that Steve and my mom, my dad, and both my brothers were able to come visit me for family weekend. As Steve's cancer was progressing, we all wanted a chance to be able to come together. The family rallied around me in support, and I told them what I had been up against since leaving home. It was a painful meeting, but one that brought us closer. I'd done the soul-searching I needed to do to heal. Once this huge family meeting was over where I was able to close the open-ended circle of the painful childhood family memories, everyone now believed me. I was able to tell everyone in my immediate family my truth and what growing up with all that shame around my abuse did to me, and they all heard me. I felt a weight lifted. This time there was no way I was going to face-plant on the ice-skating journey of my life.

Except that week after I got out of rehab—after a long day of outpatient therapy, which is a 10 a.m. to 3 p.m. sort of group therapy day program, followed by a couple of stressful haircuts at my new salon—I felt the familiar lurching of my body to act out in some way. Just because I was able to be honest with people in my life didn't mean the habits were magically cleared. Now, for the second time, I had gone to inpatient rehab, transitioned out, and relapsed.

What I really wanted to do was smoke weed, but I knew that would stay in my system for up to thirty days, and when I went back to outpatient on Monday, it would show up on the drug test. So I decided that the much smarter approach to a quick and consequence-free relapse would be to do an upper moment, because you pee that out of your system in just twenty-four hours. Because living back in rehab, spending my family's money, no phone, to sit alone in my despair, wasn't an option. The realization that the honest moment I had with my family and partner wouldn't immediately cure me was devastating, like really devastating.

What was the catalyst for my relapse, you ask? It was a mix of the "fuck its" and a chance encounter. (Fuck its are something you can catch when you have just been pushed too far outside of your threshold of tolerance, so you say "fuck it.")

Years earlier, pre-Sergei, I'd gone out with a yoga teacher who said to me on our second date, "You're so different from any guy I've ever dated."

"What do you mean?" I said.

"They all had six-packs," he said.

In all the interactions with the people I casually dated, this man hurt my feelings more deeply in much less time than it took most men. Casual body shaming by someone I really liked and had been intimate with left a lasting scar in those early twenties of mine. And of all the people in the world, I ran into that same yoga teacher from those years before. His apartment was on my drive home from rehab and my addict Spidey-sense alerted me that his presence was near at a random stoplight in West Hollywood. I turned to my left and there he was. Into the car he jumped.

We figured out pretty quickly what trouble we would be getting into. He pulled out a bag and a pipe. We went out all night. I cheated on Sergei relentlessly again, but this time, unlike the first time I had done meth, I stayed and acted out sexually. When I dropped the yoga teacher off at his house, he looked at me.

"Do you wanna lose your relationship?" he said.

"No," I said. "I don't." I was shirtless and missing a shoe but still wearing my sweatpants. In a testament to how weird a drug meth is, none of this felt at all off.

I went back to my apartment to find Sergei sitting on my doorstep.

"Something has to change," he said. And I knew he was right.

I was sure that the problem absolutely, positively had to be Los Angeles. I was surrounded by temptations and triggers.

It also so happened that through my inherent skankitude, I had gotten us bedbugs in our West Hollywood apartment and that was just one too many things. Not to mention, Steve's condition was rapidly deteriorating, and I wanted to be closer to my family.

Somehow, I convinced Sergei—and myself—that we should move to St. Louis. It was close enough to Quincy for us to be a bigger part of my family's life, but far enough away that it wasn't that impending sense of doom—oh my God, I'm going back to the place that I spent seventeen years desperately trying to escape.

Steve always told me that no matter where you go, there you are. But I was utterly convinced that if we just made a clean break, everything would be different.

And it was. We moved to St. Louis and my sexual compulsivity magically cleared, like the world's acne.

Steve beat his cancer.

Voldemort was never to be seen or heard from again.

And the next ninety-nine pages of this book are blank, for you to journal about your thoughts on the book. Maybe you could decoupage some of your favorite actresses. Or color! Just, like, make it your own and personalize it.

Okay, that's not what happened.

It's about to get dark. And because it's about to get so dark, here's a cute little sixth-grade report I did on Bill Clinton. Enjoy!

(Monica, you are an amazing person and I'm sorry for what you went through. You are an incredibly brave, fierce person.)

The Bill Clinton Sex Scandal

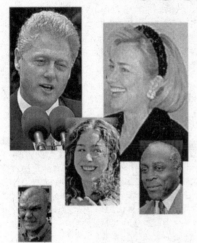
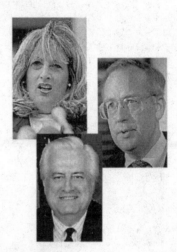
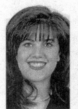
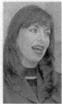
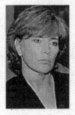

According to Me

By Jack Van Ness

I'm sure you've heard of Bill Clinton, Monica Lewinsky, Paula Jones and Kathleen Willey. But it seems to me that only important politicians and grown up get input on this. But kids also form a strong opinion. I will tell you mine and some other kids in my classes.

I will tell you the four stages I went through and some other section thoughts. But there's a catch. It's all written by an 11-year-old sixth grader. If you think anything's offensive, remember freedom of speech. My goal is to inform grown ups that kids have a strong opinion and that what grown ups do does have a strong impact on me and on my friends and on the youth of America.

Personal Thoughts

These are my personal thoughts on the Bill Clinton sex scandal. Before all of

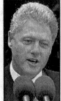

Clinton

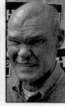

Carville

this stuff came about, I was a conservative Democrat. I thought this country was in good shape, economically speaking. Then when all of this came about , I went through four stages which were; shock, impact, shut-up and ridiculous. Now as it stands, I have turned independent. I also think Bill Clinton is a scumbag just like his friend James Carville.

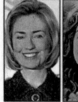

Hillary

Chelsea

I honestly don't think Bill Clinton would have ever done this if he knew what would happen. I don't think anybody in their right mind would do something like that if they knew what would happen. But still no matter how you slice it, what he did was, is and will always be wrong and immoral. Now as to Hillary, you go girl. You too Chelsea.

Now as to what I want to happen is Clinton to be impeached or to resign. But I have a feeling he doesn't have the guts to resign and then my gut feeling is he will not be impeached.

Shock

One quiet morning, I was watching the Today Show as usual and then suddenly all this was reported and it put me in "shock". I just could not believe that somebody whom I looked up to and admired did something like that. But, at first I thought it was a lie, all a rumor. But I guess I was wrong. I guess I also refused to believe it. That was about the last thing in the world I ever expected to happen. I thought it would all just blow over in a matter of days. But it has been going on for more than eight long months. And it will probably go on for another eight months. That's what I think is shocking.

Point in Time

Linda Tripp, tape recorder, the thick of Paula Jones, the Monica Lewinsky case just exposed.

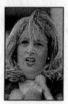
Tripp

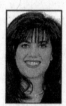
Lewinsky

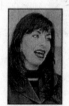
Jones

Impact

The impact on me was great and probably so for the rest of the USA. This was a huge "impact" on the news. I guess I was still a little in "shock". All I could hear about was blue dress, immunity and so on and so forth. My generation will probably never understand what all this was until we're grown making an impact on us while we wait.

We kids need role models. I had many, one being Bill Clinton. We should be in awe of people like them. But for the thousands of thousands of kids who had him as a role model, we were disgusted. We had to drop one of our role models and find a new one.

Before all of this we were really getting the image of the United States up there. I thought this country was doing great until somebody wrecked it. Who you ask? None other than the highest person in the USA. The President of the United States of America, Bill Clinton. Talk about impact, he made a big, big, bad impact. He made so many parents who had no money to spend or spare pay a ton of tax money because he was sex hungry.

Shut Up

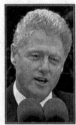

Clinton

By now everything was consumed by this including myself. Bill kept on lying and Ken Starr would not be quiet. I know I wanted them to just shut up. My mind was dominated by this. I had dreams about this because this is all I heard about. The news was almost always just about this. I don't know one person who wanted Ken Starr to keep on talking. I sure didn't. Now I'm not trying to shift the blame on Ken Starr, but he just seemed to be

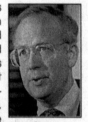

Starr

dragging this all out, just to annoy us. Please Ken, please, just shut up.

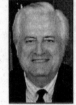

Hyde

Point in time

Blue Dress, testimony, cigar, Henry Hyde and the Starr report.

Ridiculous

Now with all of this going on, I guess Ken and Bill didn't realize that's not all that's going on in the world. The Tanzanian and Kenyan bombings, Pakistan and India's nuclear testing, important person's deaths and everyday presidential responsibilities.

Some of my estimates are if you have your average news program, 25% of it was stuff other than Bill Clinton. 75% was Bill Clinton sex scandal things. So many things needed more attention that the White House and its officials basically blew off.

This thing got so ridiculous when we bombed Pakistan believing they were making weapons of mass destruction they thought this was to divert attention off of Bill Clinton. I don't mean to blame it on others but come on, please!

Impact on kids around the USA
according to me

I'm sure a lot of kids went through what I did. But so many kids had to drop one role model and find a new one. To see somebody who we looked up to do this sets one of the worst examples for us. And he says he loves the youth of America, then why did he do this? That question bewilders me. This made a huge impact on kids around the USA.

Amazingly, some people still liked him. Unfortunately for Bill, it was mostly Democrats who basically had to.

He caused a national disgrace, discouraged the people trying to make this country a better one. The impact of his actions will be felt more by my generation in years to come.

Other Kids Actual Opinions

Some kids wish to remain anonymous, so no kids names will be released. I asked approximately 20 kids about their opinions on this matter. Kids called him everything from a scumbucket to a jerk. 19 of the 20 kids surveyed strongly don't like him. The one person who said he liked him thinks he "just made a mistake". 95% of the class wants him impeached or to resign.

One girl said, "He should resign while he still has some pride left. He is a coward for not telling the truth in the first place."

One of the intelligent responses was, "he needs to really think before he does inappropriate things and really think about the country he supposedly loves."

The bottom line is, Bill Clinton is not liked with the kids in Quincy, Illinois.

As I told you in the introduction, I had many goals in writing this. I hope I have reached them.

My main goal I really wanted to achieve was that I wanted people to know that kids have a <u>very</u> strong opinion. Also something about views on current events, which I hope I have shown you.

I thought this matter was cooling down until they releases the Tripp tapes and the impeachment inquiries.

I hope you have learned something about my views.

My suggestion to you, Bill Clinton, is to get your act together because the kids <u>will not wait</u> for you to make another mistake.

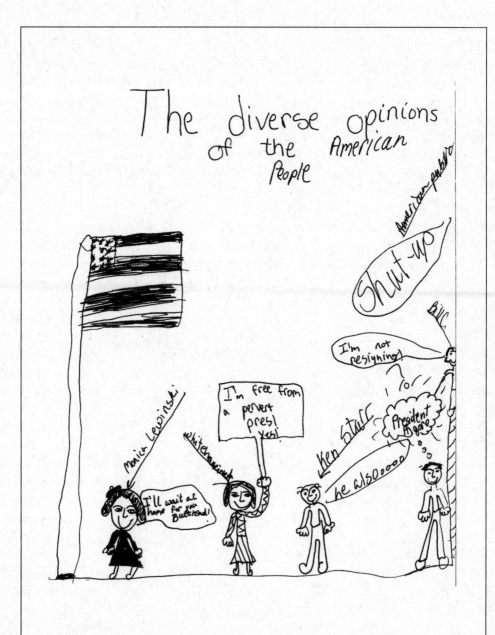

CHAPTER 9

JONATHAN AND THE NO GOOD, VERY BAD SUMMER

PICTURE THIS: I'M IN THE BATHROOM. SITTING AT MY FEET IS MY precious baby cat, Bug. I'm getting ready for the majesty of what was probably the fifth stranger eggplant of the day. Bug is looking incredulously up at me as I dance around in place, waiting to evacuate the cleansing water. I know exactly what he's thinking. *Are you serious? Can you put your balloon down for long enough to pet me and feed me? Can you make it a day without taking a different D? Is there a soul in there? How about let's turn our phone off, tell that man he's not coming over, and order some nice takeout and stop this nightmare. If not, I'm going to call your mother. You've been shaking naked in the corner holding a box of azithromycin on and off for weeks now. I'm gonna need you to get it together, girl.*

I learned as a yoga teacher that you should never lie to your students. If you say you're going to do something one more time on each side, you better do things one more time on each side. So in that spirit of honesty, I apologize to you when I said everything was magically cleared after I moved to St. Louis. Because actually, things got worse.

We arrived in St. Louis in a truly gorgeous time of year, when there was 105 percent humidity with no end in sight. Sergei got a job working retail, but we hoped that with my family's local connections he would be able to eventually get a better job. Unfortunately that never did end up happening. We had hoped moving to a smaller job market with lower cost of living would help us succeed and lower stress. In reality we both took pay cuts, and somehow between moving and reestablishing ourselves we actually were more stressed and more strapped financially. I got a rental studio to build a hair clientele out of, because it's always smart to move to a new city with no clients and get a job at a salon that has no walk-ins and is rental based with again literally no foot traffic whatsoever. Sounds like a recipe for success if you ask drug-addled, psychotically depressed Jonathan.

Let's talk about that psychotically depressed me for a moment. Part of the problem was my basic neurochemistry. I had been on antidepressants for a year with the therapist I'd been seeing, and I wasn't emotionally mature enough to understand how they'd been affecting me—that the effects were subtle but still important. I'd thought they were going to be a magic pill, and when they weren't, I decided I didn't need them anymore and stopped taking them cold turkey not long after I arrived in St. Louis. That's when I truly snapped.

A week after we got to St. Louis, my brother got married. Sergei and I drove up to Quincy for the wedding and it became clear that Steve was, at this point, locked in a fight for his life to an extent that I hadn't realized. The cancer had spread to his brain. The stereotactic radiation was no longer working to beat back the spots of cancer that kept popping up. Shortly after my brother's wedding, Steve's doctors decided that a full brain radiation would be the best course of action to get ahead of this stubborn bladder cancer that kept popping up in his brain.

The next week, they did the full brain radiation on Steve and he was never the same. My mom called me and asked for Sergei and me to come up to Quincy because Steve had had a really bad reaction to the radiation and a large portion of his scalp had been burned and fallen off. And when I say his scalp had fallen off, I mean off. To the fascia. Two days after the full brain radiation, he had acquired an infection that went through his scalp down into his torso that rendered him unable to tolerate any more chemo. His blood cell count plummeted. And for three weeks, he couldn't take chemo and tumors were seemingly popping up overnight—on his chest, on his neck, everywhere.

The hardest thing about losing a loved one to cancer is when the tide starts to turn and you know that you're getting beat and you know how serious each minute has become. The team of doctors kept trying to search for the source of the infection, but they couldn't get it under control. By the time they finally found an antibiotic that would control it, Steve's blood count had left him in a state where the only option left was palliative care.

With that, they made the gut-wrenching decision to bring him home.

When you're in hospice, the goal is to alleviate any pain and suffering on your way out the door. And to that end, they use morphine. Steve had been sober for twenty-eight years. Having to dose him every day closer toward death ... There are no words to describe the heartache of watching your hard-fought sober dad be dosed, unconsciously, with morphine. However hard it was for me, I can't begin to find the words here that would do justice to the otherworldly heart-wrenching pain that this caused our family.

A day after we got Steve home, our church choir and all Steve's closest friends came by to say their goodbyes. Steve experienced his first day pain-free in months, getting to see all his friends and family he'd been separated from while he was fighting like an animal for his life. It gave him those gorgeous chemicals that our brains create when we connect with people, making him think maybe he'd made a mistake, and that he'd given in too soon. We talked to his team again about maybe going back on chemo. They said this was really normal—when you come into hospice thinking that maybe you can go back and fight it. But it's not real.

"You two should go back to St. Louis. The doctors think it's going to be a couple weeks," my mom said.

"Okay," I said. Sergei had a couple interviews he wanted to take and I had to do some clients, so we decided to go back to St. Louis.

Before I left to drive back, my mom said to me, "Steve's going to die on our wedding anniversary. I just know it."

"That's never going to happen," I said.

The next week was their anniversary. That morning, my mom called. "You need to come home," she said. I had just started my first client. "Steve's gonna go today."

I dropped the phone and started to cry. The girl whom I shared my rental room with looked at me. "What's wrong?" she said.

"That was my mom," I said. "My stepdad's gonna die today."

"Hold on a minute," she said. She dropped down and pulled four Klonopin out of her purse. "You're gonna need this," she said.

I went home and called my cousin, who said she was on her way to St. Louis to pick me up. I popped a Klonopin and packed a few days' worth of clothes. As I got in Alexis's car, the lightening and intoxicating effects of the Klonopin began to kick in. To my surprise, all of a sudden, Steve's impending demise felt overshadowed by the tasty allure of a Texas sheet cake at Walmart, and also by the number 7 combo meal at Taco Bell, both of which I forced Alexis to stop on the way home to get. It was like if I could invent any more stops before I got home to Quincy, it would just put another fifteen minutes between me and watching Steve lose this fight.

When we walked into the house, Steve was in a hospital bed in the living room, where he used to sit in his chair. Everyone was there: both of my brothers and their wives, my stepsister, and both of my grandparents.

I sat numbly, eating my Taco Bell. My brother left to go get some ingredients to make guacamole. Our grief was leading us all toward Mexican food.

It was five o'clock. Sixteen years ago, I thought, right now, we were all taking pictures in little tuxedos, and my cousin was in her champagne-colored bridesmaid dress, and my mom was in her wedding dress, and we were getting ready to become a bigger family. Now I was listening to my stepdad begin to make the early sounds of the death rattle, which is when your lungs are dying and begin to fill up with fluid.

"It's happening," my stepsister said. Before you go into hospice they give you a book telling you what to expect from the death process. Steve had slowly but surely checked off every-thing on the list, one by one, to my horror. Picking at his clothes. Talking to people who weren't there. Bouts of anger. The death rattle was the next thing on the list.

We gathered around and held hands. "Let's say the Lord's Prayer," my mom said.

After we said it, in unison holding hands around him, my mom said, "Lord Jesus, Steve has fought the good fight. Send your legion of angels down and take him home so he can stop suffering." When she said that, we all went around in a circle one by one and said our goodbyes to Steve. When it came back to my mom, she said, "Take him home." And with those words, on his side, he took one more little inhale and that was it.

Everyone just bent over. My grandma fell on the couch. My stepsister threw herself on him. My mom turned and ran into the bathroom. I followed her. She was waving her hands in her face. "I can't believe this is happening," she said in agony. I watched her as she paced back and forth. "I can't believe this is happening," cringing with every word.

She wiped her tears away, walked back to the kitchen, and called hospice right away. Within five minutes, a team of three hospice nurses were in the house, collecting the morphine. My mom didn't leave Steve's side. Their dog, Abby, this Goldendoo-dle they'd adopted together six years prior, wouldn't leave his side either. But for the rest of us, seeing them move him onto his back and put him into a body bag was too much. So we went into the front room and we waited. A half an hour went by. It was six o'clock, which was exactly when their wedding had finished sixteen years earlier.

I heard the wheels of the stretcher carrying Steve start to move. I heard Abby's paws follow right behind all the way to the front door. She would sit there for three days, waiting for him to come back.

I went outside, calling Sergei, screaming for him to come to Quincy. He said he had to work and he would be there the next day. There was nothing he could do.

At the end of that day, when the person I'd loved and put through unspeakable pain couldn't show up for me, that was the instant where I went from psychotically depressed to truly not caring if I woke up the next day.

As I sit and write this now, all these years later, with all the work that I've done and everything I've been through, I care so deeply about myself and what happens to me and what happens to my body and who I let appreciate it. There's a self-respect that I have fought so hard for since that day. But as much as I care about myself today, I felt the complete opposite then. There was nothing so bad and nothing so reckless that I didn't think I deserved it.

* * *

Steve was gone and I was shattered. After the funeral, we went back to St. Louis. I was completely numb, two months into cold-turkey antidepressant withdrawal. Completely empty. I wasn't suicidal in a classic sense, but I didn't have a bone in my body that cared about what happened to me—if I overdosed on some drug, or ended up in the house of somebody who killed me, or got any kind of disease. I didn't care. I didn't know who I was anymore, but I knew where I needed to go.

Sergei was coming home one day just as I was leaving. "Where are you going?" he asked.

"Oh, just to go do a house call," I said. For my nonexistent clientele.

My "house call" was actually another instance of sexual acting-out behavior. After sufficiently retraumatizing myself, adding copious amounts of drugs to the equation, I went straight to the bathhouse. I had realized the depths of my own Jekyll and Hyde. I was hurting myself in such an extreme way that I had effectively put my soul through a food processor.

I'd been there for a couple hours, looking for other people in the throes of their addictions, seeking the dark energy of validation and light of day the world had denied us. It's not real validation—it's poison validation that slowly eroded our souls. I was drunk on that poison. She was Sodom and Gomorrah in St. Louis, Missouri.

Roaming from room to room, from dark hallway to dark

hallway, from one anonymous partner to the next, with my eyes fixed at a downward forty-five-degree angle, I saw the bottom half of a clothed body. I looked up and it was Sergei. His eyes were huge and studded with tears. He looked horrified.

"Come home," he said.

"What are you doing here?"

"You don't need to be here," he pleaded.

"Get out," I said. "Please go. I'm not coming home."

"Come home," he said. "Please come home."

He picked me up. I was trying to shove him off me. Finally, he put me down.

"I have to go collect my things," I said. Shaking off Sergei, I popped off into one more stranger's room for one last hoorah. The lengths to which I went in my grief and addiction surprised even me, but even more surprising was that no matter what I did to myself I couldn't feel anything. I no longer had feelings, I had turned into pain, I had turned into suffering. I had nothing left to give. When I was finished, Sergei met me outside and we went home.

I don't know if it was the relentless battle against sexual compulsivity that I was facing, or the misery we were both enduring in St. Louis, but Sergei had had enough. He and my mom sat me down and told me that she would be financing his move back to Los Angeles and that he and I were done. I was crushed. I knew that Sergei and I were in a really bad place, but

I thought in light of everything that had happened with Steve, he would give me one more chance.

He couldn't.

He moved back to Los Angeles. And I stayed behind, coming at my inner child with every sharp object I could find.

Maybe the solution was that I needed some other kind of rehab. I found a weird outpatient twelve-step therapy in my hometown, only instead of a general "higher power," the God of your choosing had to be Jesus.

On my first day, the leader of the program looked at me. "Lemme ask you something, son," he said. "Do you believe that Jesus could deliver you from your homosexuality?"

"I'm gonna go get Starbucks," I said and beelined for the door and never went back.

* * *

Between me and Sergei ending, Steve's death, and the stress of moving across the country, I got sick. And I don't get sick often, but when I get sick, I get sick.

I had an appointment set with one of my four loyal clients in St. Louis, but I was so sick I thought there was virtually no chance of me making it through. My head was pounding and my throat was sore. Still, I knew I couldn't cancel on her. She was one of the best clients I had, and she made me feel like I wasn't a total flop.

When I got to the salon, I felt faint and dizzy but I was sure that I could power through it. All of a sudden, I saw stars and felt my body collapse. The next thing I knew, her tray was beside me, I was faceup on the ground with hairdressers standing over me, and my client was crying. I had fully passed out, flat-as-a-board, in the middle of doing her buttery blond highlights.

Waking up, I immediately thought: *Oh no. This feels like a story that I've heard before. This is that flu that just won't go away. This is that persistent fever. But maybe it's not. I've been in front of the firing squad before and always come out fine.* I had already taken a Z-pack. I knew I had to go to Planned Parenthood and get tested.

I scraped myself off the ground and a friend said she would finish doing my client's hair. I went home and went to sleep.

The next day, I went to Planned Parenthood and asked for a full STD panel. In the little exam room, a nurse came in. She told me the rules of the rapid test, which I'd heard multiple times before. Then she swabbed my mouth. She said she'd be back in ten minutes.

Ten minutes turned into fifteen. Fifteen minutes turned into twenty. Twenty minutes turned into thirty. My heart began to sink.

I heard shuffling outside the closed waiting room door of what sounded like several pairs of feet. There was a faint knock.

"Can I come in?" the nurse said gently. In after her walked two other women who seemed fidgety and nervous.

Suddenly it dawned on me: These were all girls in training and this was the first HIV+ test result they'd had. They wanted the girls to sit in on the appointment to see how it was done.

"Do you mind if these trainees observe while we discuss your results?"

"Yes," I said. Tears sprung into my eyes. "Yes, I absolutely fucking mind. No, they can't sit in here. Please, get out."

The trainees looked chastened. They left in silence.

The nurse sat down next to me. Quiet tears were streaming down my face. I looked down at my green cargo shorts, wiping my tears on them.

When I looked up, she was looking at me. "You have a preliminary positive result for HIV," she said. The dam broke and I started to sob.

She told me that they needed to take a little bit more blood to send to the lab and that I would need to go to a specialist they would refer me to for further testing. With that initial blood sample, they confirm that you are definitely positive, and that it's not a false positive, and they identify what strain you have and if you have any mutations.

She showed me a disclaimer printed out on a sheet of paper and explained it to me. It said that as of this date of that year, if you had sex with someone and don't inform them of your

HIV status, you're considered a bioterrorist, and it's a felony. She had me sign it. My hand shook as I held the pen.

Then she started talking about the appointment for my follow-up. At that point, everything faded into gray.

"Can I go home now?"

I shakily walked to my car, got in, and was driving home, and I realized that my car was shaking because my hands were so unsteady as I held the steering wheel. I pulled over and called a family member.

"Don't tell anyone what I'm about to tell you," I said. "But I have HIV. Please do not tell my mom. Please do not tell anyone."

The family member said, "Call me as soon as you get home," and I promised that I would.

Thirty seconds later, my phone rang. I looked down and it was my mom.

Crying.

One moment after that, both my brothers called, one after another. Crying.

Within minutes, every single person in my family had called me in belligerent states of duress.

My mom informed me that she had just downed her bottle of Kaopectate and would be sitting on the toilet for the next six hours because she had a colonoscopy the next day, so my brother got in the car to drive to St. Louis. I was stuck waiting for him to arrive.

That day was just as devastating as you would think it would be. But at the same time, I had this sense of relief—that the lifelong fear I'd had, since I was a six-year-old boy, was finally over. The monster under the bed that had been chasing me for so long, that I had been so desperate to avoid, had finally caught me.

Everything had changed. Yet everything was much the same. I smoked a joint and ordered a shitload of my favorite Mexican restaurant takeout and got a liter of white cheese dip, then ate it all with my brother.

My worst nightmare had been realized, and I was still here.

For my first follow-up appointment a week later, my mom asked if she could come. I said that was okay but only if she didn't cry or make a scene.

My doctor was a cute little Filipino lady. The first thing I remember asking her is: "Do you think I still could live to be seventy-five?" I was twenty-five at the time.

The doctor chuckled. "I'll keep you alive long enough to die of cancer or a heart attack like everybody else," she said. She informed me that HIV treatment has come a long way and it is no longer a terminal illness, but a chronic one that is relatively easily managed with daily medication. In fact, she said, nowadays life expectancy is fifty to seventy-five years from diagnosis. I was just thinking, *Shit, I could still turn this around*, when...

I heard a thud and turned my head to see my mom falling off the chair onto the floor, fully sobbing but trying not to. She was crying so hard that no noise was coming out except for a dog-whistlelike squeak. Her face was purple like she was suffocating.

"Anne!" I snapped. I always call her that—by her mom's name—when she is being in any way extra, in the way that her mom was to her. "Go to the waiting room! You promised you wouldn't make a scene!" Like a cute little gray-haired puppy, she tilted her head, as if acknowledging that she'd bitten off more than she could chew in coming to the appointment at all. She waited for me out in the lobby. Again let me just say how much I love my mom, and I'm so sorry I put you through so much—you are the best mom I could've ever asked for.

I got about seventy-five vials of blood drawn that day. With the blood work they had done, the doctor could determine exactly how far the virus had progressed, and all the different medications that could work to stop it in its tracks. At the time, there were numerous families of medications, and my virus was able to be controlled by any one of them. We decided on one that was an all-in-one drug, so it was just a once-a-day pill. With that antiretroviral prescription, in two weeks' time I was undetectable.

I think that's super important to note here. Within just two weeks of being on medication, HIV was undetectable in my blood. People who achieve and maintain an undetectable viral load have effectively no risk of sexually transmitting the virus to an HIV-negative partner.

"Undetectable" is a term that applies to many people living with HIV. An undetectable HIV viral load means there are so few copies of the virus in your blood that the test cannot detect them.

Even the CDC (Centers for Disease Control and Prevention) agrees that a person with an undetectable viral load effectively poses no risk of transmitting the HIV virus through unprotected sex. An HIV-positive mother with an undetectable viral load can even deliver her baby with less than 1 percent risk of transmission, as long as the mother takes HIV medicine daily throughout pregnancy, and the baby takes it for four to six weeks after birth. The mother thing doesn't totally pertain to me—I just think it's incredible how far we've come in HIV/AIDS treatment.

Knowing all of that and communicating it is difficult. Sometimes it feels like I'm convincing people I'm okay, or "clean," or "safe." It's always best to do your own research; all the facts are out there.

Once I was undetectable, I was no longer at risk of infecting anyone. And I knew I hadn't infected Sergei because we only had protected sex, and I knew that any chance of his risk of exposure was none, because we hadn't been sexual in a very long time. Once I found out I was positive, I never held back my HIV status from my sexual partners. No matter how clunky and no matter how many dates or sexual encounters it meant I wasn't having. The people who pose the greatest risk for HIV transmission are people who have been exposed to the virus, have developed the infection, but are not on medication. Their viral loads can be very high, which means they are contagious. This is why HIV education and access to testing continue to be so important.

When it comes to HIV transmission, certain sexual practices put you at greater risk of infection after exposure—namely, if you're on the receiving end of anal or vaginal penetrative sex. Clutch your pearls as you may, Aunt Lydia or Susan, but these are the types of conversations that must be destigmatized in order for us to reduce HIV and AIDS and increase sexual health in general.

The culture of education and knowledge around HIV is two different worlds pre- and post-PrEP in my view. PrEP, or pre-exposure prophylaxis—a once-a-day medication that can prevent HIV infection in HIV-negative people—would hit the market months after I was infected. I have lived with the virus through that time and the extent to which it's been destigmatized since then is heartening.

Still, I've been dropped like a hot sack of potatoes because of my status. I once dated a guy for a month without having sex because I liked him so much and I wanted him to really get to know me. When I told him, he never spoke to me again.

Then again, I might have done the same thing. I'll never forget the first time a big muscle daddy came to my house to hook up when I was twenty years old and he told me he was positive. I told him I couldn't do it.

I look back at all the people who have lived with, dated with, struggled with, and come to terms with HIV and my heart bleeds with gratitude and empathy. So many of them didn't live to see the privilege of getting to survive as an HIV+ person. It's one reason why, as a thirty-two-year-old living with HIV, with the privilege and microphone I now have, I rail against the way this country's government responded—and continues to respond—to the HIV/AIDS crisis. It is one of the biggest losses of life in American history. So many people let it happen right in front of their faces and didn't lift a finger to help. So often queer people are the butt of a joke or seen as disposable. Our lives aren't valued.

I've had access to medication that's allowed me to live a long life where I can fulfill all my hopes and dreams. If I didn't know that I was HIV+, I would never know that I was HIV+. What I mean by that is: I take a pill every day now, and I see a doctor every three months, but other than that, I've done nothing but get cuter, realize my dreams, look better topless than I've ever looked before, and my new figure-skating curves? Don't even get me started. Postdiagnosis, I've accomplished more than many HIV-negative people will ever have the chance to do.

We've made huge strides because of Ryan White, Princess Diana, Elizabeth Taylor, and countless other activists, like Ruth Coker Burks, who have given so much to make up for all the people who sat around and watched it happen. And for all the hardships that I put my family through, they never let me go. Even after I got HIV, they never cast me out on the street. So many others didn't have the same love and acceptance for their own loved ones with HIV.

There's so much more work that has to be done around this conversation, and that's part of why I'm telling you this now, as hard as it is.

In a lot of this country, you can be treated as a felon for living with HIV. Someone can have their whole world turned upside down because of archaic laws that are written to criminalize and demonize people with HIV—whether it's people being harassed or incarcerated, or being denied refugee status based on their HIV. There are too many outdated laws and regulations that negatively impact and further stigmatize people living with HIV. We need to see policy that reflects the modern medical understanding of what living with HIV/AIDS is. HIV is a health issue—not a criminal one, and not a moral one. Anyone can get it.

Homosexuality and HIV stigmatization is a big problem in the United States and all over the world. In places like Chechnya, the Middle East, parts of Africa, Asia, and even in the US—where homosexuality and HIV/AIDS are so rampantly stigmatized that it can be nearly impossible to get medication, and as misinformation is pervasive—the spread of disease is on the rise. The CDC and the *New York Times* have done incredible work on the silent stigma ravaging the American South. HIV doesn't care; it affects everyone. But with what we know, we can stop the suffering HIV is causing.

My HIV infection would end up helping me learn to love myself so much more than I ever had before. When I got HIV, I felt that I wasn't allowed to be seen as sexy or desirable. I had to work so much harder to fall in love with and accept where I'd come to in my life, and forgive myself for all the decisions I'd made to get there. That wasn't an overnight process. It was a daily one. To a lesser degree, even today, it still is. Life is so much a daily exercise in learning to love yourself and forgive yourself, over and over.

Of course, it meant that my St. Louis experiment had failed and would turn out to be just a blip—and a pretty ugly mistake at that. But, hey, Nancy Kerrigan didn't give up in '94 when she was attacked with a metal police baton.

Much like Nancy, I had a lot of work to do for the life Olympics that I never could have known was waiting for me back in Los Angeles.

I'd hit bottom. Now it was time to rebuild.

CHAPTER 10

THE KHALEESI WITHIN*

*Except That Whole Unfortunate Ending

BEFORE I MOVED BACK TO LA, I PULLED OFF PERHAPS THE GREATEST heist (of my own money) the world has ever seen. *Ocean's 8* had nothing on me. My grandfather had gifted me some money. (Enough to buy a sensible vehicle. Not, like, a house. But holy mother of gratitude, did this gesture ever save my ass.) The catch was: I didn't have autonomy over that money until I was thirty-five. But I could get some—with permission—starting at twenty-five. That could amount to a few thousand dollars per year, depending on how good a year it was for advertising.

I knew come hell or high water, Los Angeles was the keyholder to my future. But my family thought that the key to my future was having COBRA health insurance, working in the basement of the newspaper in my hometown, and being close enough to family that they could peel me off the floor if I died of full-blown AIDS. *Not me, not now!* I thought to myself.

So with the poise and strength of Michelle Kwan in the 2001 World Championships, I collected myself and sauntered into my uncle's office. He happened to be my grandpa's money manager.

"Hi, Uncle Dominik!" I said breezily. "Papa left a message with your secretary—I came in to get a check for five thousand five hundred dollars from my account. That was my Christmas present this year."

He looked at me, unsure. But I assured him that we had all discussed it and the lack of message from my grandfather was just a holiday oversight.

I tapped my toe with a growing angst as his secretary brought me my check. I took it, went straight to Bank of America, deposited the check, packed up my Kia Rio, called my mom, told her that I was done in St. Louis—oops, sorry, love you, mean it, bye!—and I was back to California.

Sergei, understanding my plight, helped me to get together a bachelor apartment in West LA. I wanted to be out of the fray of West Hollywood with wider streets and less parking meter pressure. I lived in a ten-foot-by-ten-foot studio with a kitchenette that had a minifridge, a stovetop burner, a shower that I had to wash half my body in at a time, and I paid $800 for the privilege of it. That was what I could afford.

I knew that I didn't have a ton of money to last me for very long and I needed to make like McKayla Maroney at the 2012 Summer Olympics and vault myself into a successful hair clientele as soon as possible. So I started emailing and calling any clients I still had and found a cute little salon in Venice to rebuild from.

One of the first people I called was Erin Gibson. Erin is a successful writer and comedian who, years earlier, I had poached as a color client while I was working at Tonia Skoekenkaya Tutberidze. When we first met, she was doing her own color out of a box—which had worked for her until she gave herself fluorescent orange roots.

"Erin, why do you have this gorgeous haircut with such angry roots?" I asked her that day.

"I'm not paying those outrageous color prices!" she said.

I told her I would do her roots for fifty bucks out of my house at night after I got home from the salon. So she started coming over to my place one Thursday a month so I could touch up her color. She was a headshot photographer on the side, and I always asked for her advice on things—how she had become successful, and how she'd navigated her life so far.

Not long before I'd left LA for St. Louis, I'd told Erin that I wanted to make a website, and that I'd do her hair for free if she took cute headshots of me for it. I promised her three root touchups in exchange for her services. But after the first one, I bounced for St. Louis without finishing the job, even though she'd already taken the pictures of me. It nagged at me, that I'd done her dirty like that.

At my new salon on Abbot Kinney in Venice, I was stressed to show them that I could deliver clients. Erin was my last client of the day that first day. Since I'd left for St. Louis like a ghost in the night without saying goodbye, I wasn't sure if that had left a bad taste in her mouth. But as soon as I saw her, she hugged me and it was like no moments had passed since we'd seen each other last. Our friendship picked up right where it left off.

We made small talk. She asked me what had happened in St. Louis, and I told her the cold hard truth: that I'd been introduced to a total bitch named methamphetamine. We'd hung out a handful of times, had our fifteen minutes in the sun (and by sun I mean scorched earth hellfire), but those few times were enough for me to be introduced to her *other* friend, HIV. (One has a way of leading to the other.) I wasn't sure what Erin's reaction would be to me, since I hadn't told many people about this yet, but it was only one of calm compassion. Not one thing I had said had moved one hair on her head. Her ability to not see me any differently, even after that news, left me completely wigless.

As I started doing Erin's hair, my station partner, Mola-vanda, and her client started talking about *Game of Thrones*. I overheard and instantly jumped into the conversation: "Oh yeah, honey—I've been watching her. This little blond baby, she wears a sash and she's got such bad attitude, honey—she wants to kill everybody. And Christina Aguilera, honey, somebody done stole her dragons and she's mad as hell because she can't find her eggs anywhere. And then Mr. Potato Head Dr. Evil Guy, honey, he's over there doing some other stuff."

"Wait, what is this all about?" Erin said, laughing.

I shook myself out of my recapping fugue state. "What?" I said.

When Erin collected herself, she had a look on her face like she had an idea. "We need to do this for Funny or Die," she said.

"Do what?" I said.

"Recap *Game of Thrones*!"

I thought she meant doing a quick little video on our phones. I didn't realize she was talking about a full set, a full series, with lights and a crew.

* * *

Four months later, I found myself at a little salon on Melrose to tape the first two episodes of a little baby idea called *Gay of Thrones*. We didn't know exactly how it would look—if it would be a show that showed me watching *Game of Thrones*, or if it would strictly be me in a salon with a client and we would re-cap the show. In the first episode, it was basically a shocked client–played by our producer, because we didn't have a guest to play the part–getting his hair cut while I went on a tirade of incorrect pronunciations of everything on the show. It felt like it was a stream of consciousness of saying the funniest things I could think of as I recalled the first two hours of the show that I'd seen. But I hadn't really watched the show that carefully, so we were all just doing our best.

Erin tried to go through each episode before shooting and remind me of funny things I'd said, but nothing stressed me out harder than trying to learn lines. All I wanted to do was get out in front of that camera and have her yell out a scene to me, and I would riff on what had happened until we found something she liked. Then I'd do it again–shorter, tighter, faster–until the recap was perfect.

Erin took something that started off as this random thing–an off-the-cuff monologue moment from me–and turned it into something with a much more polished voice. She made it her own and got it to where it is. I definitely had a hand in build-ing it, but there was a group of people who crafted that show–nobody more so than Erin. I wouldn't be writing the words of this book right now if it wasn't for her. She and I may not talk every day, but outside of my mom, there's nobody in the world who has changed my life more than Erin Gibson has. It's crazy when I think about how much her friendship has impacted the course of my life. Even when we've had creative growing pains, we were always able to grow together, and I will always look up to her so much and strive to use my voice authentically because of the opportunity that she created for me. (And if you haven't read her book, *Feminasty: The Complicated Woman's Guide to Surviving the Patriarchy Without Drinking Herself to Death*, you should read it, because it's smart and stunning. Just like Erin.)

Anyway, about halfway through the season, I went out on a Saturday night with my girlfriends. All the girls told me they were doing molly that night, and it was no big deal—it was just two hours, all you had to do was take a teeny-tiny little pill, and you'd feel totally great and normal.

"Perfect!" I said. Remember that whole two-steps-forward-one-back thing?

At nine thirty that night, I took the molly. Great idea, I know. Three hours later, I was gone. My eyes were seven-eighths of my face. I looked like a late '90s alien. I was in the corner of my apartment watching what looked like brick walls opening and closing, hearing weird voices in my head in the accents of local newscasters I remembered from my childhood, flashing back to everyone I'd ever had sex with but wished I hadn't.

I looked over at the clock. Suddenly it was eleven thirty in the morning. I had to be on set at five thirty that evening. "Girl,"

I whispered to myself. "Go to sleep." I had been up the whole night. The minutes inched by.

Finally, I called my friend Helenskaya from rehab. Helenskaya had been horrifically addicted to meth–like hardcore, gnarly Iowa meth–and when I first met her, I'd helped her take out these really gross beaded braids she'd had put in when she was trying to get sober two years earlier. They were such a tangled mess, it was a miracle we didn't just have to cut them out. But Helenskaya had stayed sober ever since and turned into a gorgeous thriving lawyer. I knew she'd know what to do.

"Helenskaya, girl," I said. "I accidentally did this weird molly and my jaw feels like it's locked and my pupils are all crazy and I can't come down. What do I do?"

"Girl," she said, "the first thing you're gonna do is you're gonna go get you a cheeseburger with a lot of cheese and a lot of bacon on it."

"Okay," I said, exhaling.

"Then, you're gonna go get you a nice cup of 2 percent milk and you're gonna drink all of that."

"Okay."

"You're gonna go get in the shower, girl, and after that you're gonna feel like a whole new woman. And when you go out into the world, you just gotta distract from your face so nobody notices that you're all fucked up and shit."

"Got it!" I said. "Gotta go!"

I ran to Hardee's and got a double bacon cheeseburger and a 2 percent milk. I chugged the milk. I devoured the burger. I smoked a blunt. I started to come down. But still not enough.

Finally, I realized that the most genius thing I could ever do was tie my hair into a topknot, then back-comb the topknot into the biggest possible top bun, then take the longest scarf that I could find and tie it into an asymmetrical side-bow. Then, I thought, nobody would notice that my pupils were the size of my face and my eyes were completely black.

When I arrived to Funny or Die for our shoot, Erin met me outside. I was forty minutes late, with a big-ass scarf in my hair.

When I got out of the car, she looked at me like I was insane. "Oh my God," she said. "What happened to you?"

I stammered for a minute, then confessed.

"It's okay," she said. "Let's just get you a cup of coffee, huh?"

But the craziest thing was that somehow I still nailed it. I gave a stunning performance for that episode of *Gay of Thrones*. But it was a moment for me where I learned that I was under a new sense of pressure. If I wanted to be in front of the camera, I had to start prioritizing my health and well-being above my need to fit in or have fun.

A lot of the self-inflicted wounds that I experienced in my twenties were because of situations that I found myself in socially where I would get stuck in this idea that I needed to be "normal." That could mean, in this case, doing a little pill of molly to be normal, because these girls I was out with could do it and seemed to suffer no consequences. Why couldn't I?

But for me, because of my trauma, if I did those things, there was a chance I could be having sex with weirdos, or making decisions that could really negatively impact my relationship with myself and further traumatize me. That was something that I resented and resisted for a long time. Letting go of that idea that I needed to be normal or that I somehow wasn't normal just because I needed to prioritize self-care to be healthy is the biggest gift I've ever given myself. Being normal is being completely unique, because nobody's the same.

Normal, honey? Who is she, anyway?

Erin and I started to pick up more momentum out of that first season. We had developed an idea for a *Gay of Thrones* spinoff show, but it was a hard sell. We sat in meetings where the executives seemingly were unable to put me in a box that they thought would work in the way my catchphrase "Where are my dragons?" worked. They didn't seem that interested in anything else we had to say.

At one of those pitch meetings, as we were pinballing off each other, doing our Tina Fey–Amy Poehler dual-creator realness act, an executive asked us about something having to do with the first season of *Game of Thrones*.

"Oh, right," I said. "Like when that crazy guy was in hard shoulder pads and that other poor lady was pregnant, honey, and she did a full coup de grâce on her boss and took her baby and did a reverse swan dive over the cliff!"

The room fell quiet. "That was *Spartacus*," somebody said. "Not *Game of Thrones*."

"Oh," I said. It turned out the reason Erin and I never really knew what was going on in the third season of *Game of Thrones* was because neither of us had seen the first two seasons. I never even really understood anything that was happening because I'd watched *Spartacus* in rehab all those years earlier—never *Game of Thrones*. But I ended up becoming a hard-core *GoT* superfan who devoured the first two seasons . . . I was just a little late to the party.

As *Gay of Thrones* continued to pick up momentum, I had been stung by the content creation bee. She's an elusive little creature. Her sting is highly addictive. Her symptoms include a constant need for creative expression, an incessant thirst for validation, and a sense of having something to say but not knowing quite how to say it. For the first time, I realized there might be something more for me than doing hair. I had a curiosity and desire to expand in a way that made me passionate and gave me a drive that I hadn't had since I was a teenager. It was my new cheerleading, my new yoga, my new mountain to climb.

When I'd first lived in Los Angeles, I had made fun of people who had moved there to become famous. I had to ask myself: *Is that something that I want now too?* But I was just excited to have a new creative outlet.

So I started working with a manager, and doing little auditions here and there, or filming sizzle reels for shows that would never get picked up but that I did anyway because I was eager to learn and create in this brave new digital world. One day a few months after working with them I got exciting news. I got my first big offer, from the Style network. But like so many fates at the big-offers graveyard, mine was vanquished when a day after we received the offer, the Style network was bought out by Esquire, rebranding it as a channel for men and squashing my deal.

"You're like the T. rex the day before the asteroid hit," my manager said.

A friend recommended me for a guest-starring part on a scripted show, but when I showed up to audition, they kept asking me to say, "Where are my dragons?" By the sixth time, I was so nervous that I forgot my lines, and then I asked for "slides" instead of "sides." Never mind that my character only had one line, which was to say, "Cupcakes!"

For years, I went on random auditions, mostly for parts like "Gay Best Friend" or "Commenting on Red Carpet Looks," but the opportunities that came my way just weren't the right vehicles for this little girl right here. I realized that I needed a safe space to create content that satisfied my curiosity and allowed me to explore my interests in a new and healthy way. That led me to start my passion project, a podcast called *Getting Curious*. My friend Clovis worked for a podcasting network and offered to help me launch *Getting Curious*. I was very new to the podcast world, and our little show was rough-and-tumble. Clovis would end up leaving the network where *Getting Curious* got its start. After about a year there, *Getting Curious* was canceled for lack of funding, which was a bummer, but I knew that the concept was something I was passionate about continuing. That's when Clovis came back in with his wife, Oxana, and helped me produce the show independently, until another network would scoop it up. I was just grateful to keep expanding my view of the world and telling stories.

There wasn't any real work for me, though, besides *Gay of Thrones*. So I continued doing hair, hoping that some bigger opportunity would come along.

"Should I have, like, an agent?" I asked my manager at one point. "Maybe we need a hosting agent on the team. There's gotta be some hosting auditions that we don't even know about. Maybe I could do, like, a John Oliver thing. Or be, like, a big gay Christiane Amanpour."

"Maybe you should take a hosting class," they said. *Ew.*

I ended up firing them. It was one of the first times in my

adult life that I'd really taken a stand, and as soon as I did, it was like jumping off the deep end for the first time.

It was scary, but also very freeing. Sometimes our insecurity and fear about being alone or independent in the world can be our Achilles' heel. I've learned that several times—and I'm not just being hard on myself. I wish my future self could go back in time and tell my younger self, "Don't be afraid to be alone, honey—you're okay. Don't do anything stupid. Just take your ass to Trader Joe's and get some oatmeal raisin cookies. Get the chocolate chip ones, too, because they will melt in your mouth. Which you will need to have a few of to soothe the amount of stress you're going to experience, queen." When the people around you believe in you and your potential wholeheartedly, you can make your dreams come true. If they believe your dreams are out of reach, you have to open the door and make your way to people who want to basket-toss your ass right into those dreams. At the end of the day, the people we let in our space affect our ability to get to where we want to go, so if they're in the way of realizing your potential, it's okay to disconnect because you must choose yourself. I used to think that was selfish but really it's just healthy.

* * *

There was always this drive to have a New York City moment. I met a guy named Gleb who brought me to New York with him for my first real trip as an adult. Gleb had previously dated a successful businessman who owned a brownstone on the Upper West Side that had a little pied-à-terre—like a bachelor apartment—where we stayed when we began going regularly. After Gleb and I broke up, he let me continue staying there, which was super generous of him (and his ex-lover). It made it possible for me to get to know the city and have it be financially feasible, because as a rental hairdresser and small business owner in LA, I couldn't leave my life there for too long. It was far from luxurious, but it was everything I needed.

As soon as I got to New York, I instantly felt like I had to live there. I wanted to move there all the way. Even the hair was different: harder and edgier, blunt and choppy. It wasn't just: "Give me highlights with blended face frames and dirty roots." It was dynamic and interesting. You would see different shapes from different eras, diversity and style. I felt inspired by the energy, the architecture, the shapes, the cultures—the whole tapestry of life in New York.

I'd always imagined it would be too overwhelming and out of my reach. But as it turned out, it was exactly where I wanted to be. I felt like a duck that had finally gotten into the right pond and was just, like, Swim, queen.

I knew a hairstylist in New York named Bronislav, who coincidentally was a dear friend of the owner of the very first salon I had ever worked at in Scottsdale. (One word to the wise there, kids: Keep in touch! You never know when you'll need someone's help.) I asked Bronislav if there was any way I could speak to the owner of his salon in New York to start building a clientele there. And so I started coming to New York for just one day every month to get a start in the city. I didn't really make any money—it was just enough for me to come for a few days, stay at that place on the Upper West Side, and get used to what New York could be. But I kept falling more and more in love with it. Every time I left, I would think: *I don't want to leave. I just want to stay here.*

That fall, I got a job hosting a daily lifestyle tech show. I was auditioning to replace somebody and I had every nerve possible. It was my first grown-up job after *Gay of Thrones*. Luckily, the producer, Lavra, was a fan, as well as a total sweetheart. It paid $300 an episode, and it was three weeks of work.

"Have you ever worked with a teleprompter?" she asked me.

"Oh my God, all the time! Teleprompter is like my middle name," I said. "I'm so, so comfortable with a teleprompter." (I had never used one before and googled how to do it immediately after.) "See you in two days, girl."

I was hardly a natural, but I figured it out pretty quickly. After three weeks of consistent on-camera work, they asked me if I wanted to extend the gig. But there wasn't a solid contract they could offer, so I would have been moving to New York with no guarantees. I would just keep coming back and forth to New York to do hair and wait for the right opportunity to come my way.

The next day, with three days left in New York, my former manager—the one I'd fired years ago—called and told me they were casting the reboot of *Queer Eye* and that I was perfect for their new logline, which he'd heard was: "Turning red states pink one makeover at a time." I thanked him for the call, hung up the phone, called my current team, and had an 8.5-level freak-out on the management-earthquake Richter-scale. "Why did my old manager just call me to tell me that a life-changing opportunity is on the table that I didn't even know about?" I said. "We have three days to assemble a pitch packet, ladies! I've got to get a meeting with them by Monday."

When I think back to that time, I see myself sitting on one of my dearest friends Poliksana's couch, defeated by one personal setback after another, trying to navigate heartbreak and loss, wondering if this was the end. I wondered if season one of *Gay of Thrones* was the end, or if season two would be, all the way up to season four, leading into an unfulfilling attempt at YouTube success, getting laughed out of auditions, and never knowing if the entertainment industry really had any room for a person like me. Maybe *Gay of Thrones* was the zenith of my entertainment content creation career.

That would have been fine—I had always loved doing hair. All my hard work honing my craft as a hairdresser had paid off.

I was working really hard to build a clientele in New York that could support me on my way to becoming a successful bicoastal hairdresser. I had spent four years with nibbles of success, a bit of popularity and a small Instagram following I kept nurturing, while I waited and wondered if a bigger break was coming.

I had spent the first half of my twenties fighting to find the will to process everything that I'd survived in my childhood and adolescence. Having done that hard work, I was now in a chapter in my life where I had the clarity to pursue my dreams and passions and find some actual success. When Sergei and I finally called it quits, I had the painful realization that for years I had only been willing to save myself or care about myself for the sake of Sergei and "us." It took him leaving once and for all for me to realize that I had been worth saving all along.

CHAPTER 11

WHO IS SHE?

I DIDN'T SHOW UP FOR MY *QUEER EYE* AUDITION IN MY BEST LOOK.

I was running there from a job, so I had my hairstyling setcase (the case of hair tools you bring to set to work) with me. I was in all black and had done my level best with a hastily packed lint roller to remove the twelve haircuts' worth of hair that I'd spent all day doing. I didn't even have time to re-zhuzh my look after work as I would have liked. I was serving five o'clock shadow realness—neck beard, far from fresh. In my mind's eye, the producers would go for a grooming expert who was masculine-presenting and least threatening to a straight audience. But as one of my best friends, Dragomira, always says: You miss 100 percent of the chances you don't take. (I'm told Wayne Gretzky was the original coiner of this quote but we all know hockey is not my ice sport of choice, so Dragomira, queen—own it.) So I brought my low-slung-bun, hippie gay-man-chic ass over to that audition. But I was pretty sure they would never cast me for it on appearance alone. (Also, in typical Jonathan fashion, my phone was 100 percent dead and I had to do a cutesy bouncy beg to get the girl at the front desk to charge it for me. I couldn't get back to the Upper West Side with a dead phone! She graciously obliged. She let me know I could take a seat on the little blue couch and it would be just a few moments before someone from casting would be out to get me.)

If you're reading this with my voice in your head, now switch the voice in your head to Moira Rose, played by Catherine O'Hara, on Dan Levy's *Schitt's Creek*.

Now: As I was nervously awaiting the producer's arrival, I looked down at my Rick Owens top and anxiously chased away the remaining hair splinters that were plaguing my décolletage. I tried to sit up a little bit straighter to cover up for the fact that I wasn't feeling quite myself about my OOTD, David.

Okay. Now it's safe to switch back to my voice.

When I sat down with the casting producer, she asked me why I thought I was right for this.

I told her the truth. "*Queer Eye* was a really big deal for me because it gave me a way to talk about my sexuality with my family that wasn't threatening," I said. "I watched it with my parents. And I loved it. Kyan was my first crush. I have an au-tographed photo of Jai under my bed." I hesitated, because I knew I had to say something potentially controversial. "I also hate the term *metrosexual*," I said. "At the time *metrosexual* was a cheeky term, but kind of problematic now because it seems to make self-care reductive and outwardly identifiable. For me, beauty is from the knowledge I've gained and how I use that knowledge to make my own individual idea of what it means to look great—find something fresh that makes me the best me I can be, not a cookie-cutter idea of a well-kept 'metrosexual.' I want to cultivate the idea that good hair and skin is from the inside out."

"What do you want to see from the new version?" she asked me.

I thought about it. "If nothing else," I said, "I just want it to be diverse. Our community has come such a long way since this came out. I just hope this version reflects that."

The next day, I found out that I'd gotten a callback. For the next round, I had to send in a self-tape, which is an audition that you record yourself. Immediately it made me very nervous because every self-tape I've ever done has been garbage. I just don't audition very well. I've also noticed this in my online dating life, that I feel like I'm so cute that I don't have to work very hard to post pictures that reflect my cuteness. I just expect everyone to see the raw beauty radiating from me. My experience with self-tapes up until that point had been being elbow-deep in a corrective color, covered in hair-color spatters, stressed within an inch of my life, blubbering through lines that are completely incorrect or from a character or situation that's not going on or called for in the self-tape at all, and submitting said self-tape, then never hearing anything ever again. But this time, that couldn't be my fate.

I really hope what I sent in to *Queer Eye* has been destroyed, because as predicted, I was sweating profusely, under horrible lighting, and extremely nervous.

But it must have worked. Because a few days later, I found out that I'd been selected for the final fifty. (This was something torn from the *America's Next Top Model* playbook, honey. I was about to be the next girl who had come up against so many nos but wouldn't take them for an answer. I was Jaslene, cycle eight winner, who had been turned away in cycle seven but came back triumphantly to take the crown. Interestingly enough, she and cycle six winner Danielle were the only two winners, that I could find, who had CoverGirl renew their contracts.) The next stage was to come in for a chemistry test, which would be a three-day audition in Glendale. The first night was at a local bar.

We got an email saying, in so many words, "This is our chance to see you guys working together, so don't be a wall-flower!"

I was basically Svetlana Khorkina in the 2000 Sydney Games. As I'm sure you recall, the vault was set too low in the all-around final, so everyone in the first rotation who was on vault had crash landings on both of their attempts—including Svetlana, who had all eyes on her, since everyone was sure she was going to win. This could be leaving her unable to come back and possibly claim gold. But then in the second rotation, an Australian gymnast noticed that the vault was over a foot too low. When the judges confirmed that everyone in the first rotation had done both of their vaults on a vault that was set at over a foot below regulation level, the judges determined that each gymnast in the first rotation would be given another chance to vault. But Svetlana was the first one to go up on the second rotation, which, in her group, was uneven bars. She was already so rattled from her experience that she fell on uneven bars, rendering her chance to revault useless because the damage was already done. I knew that I could not let all this pressure of Olympic glory derail my vaulting into the gold medal of this competition. No matter what this audition apparatus was set to—I was going to nail my vault. But also, Svetlana, I'm still so personally sorry for you.

One of the things I remember from that first night is meeting Karamo. As soon as I saw him, my vagina melted into a puddle all over his cobalt blue suit. When I found out he had a long-term boyfriend, now fiancé, my vagina resolidified and collected itself back inside my body and then I realized that we were actually ebony and ivory sisters. I didn't meet Antoni or Bobby the first night, but I saw Tan from across the room. I was so intimidated by the sheer perfection that was his bone structure, I didn't dare approach him.

The second and third day were in a ballroom of a Glendale Embassy Suites. I had heartburn the whole time—just this unmoving, burning sphere of agita right in my solar plexus. But I was also very much enjoying the process of turning it on. In our first exercise, we went table by table, group by group divided by your vertical, so ten of us in each group, talking to different people—the Netflix people, the production company people, the creators of the show. After you finished, you'd regroup with the other boys to talk about what had just happened. "What did you say?" they'd whisper. "What did they ask you?" I was meeting the other boys but mostly I was trying to save my energy for when it was my turn to do the round robin.

When they asked me about body hair, I knew just what to say. "If you want it, keep it!" I said. "Why are you waxing? Do you feel more confident? Could we do some gorgeous exfoliation and toning so we're not getting acne from our waxcapades?" My philosophy was very much to embrace yourself and love what you are, instead of making you something you're not. Refine what you already have—don't change it at its core. That's always been my whole ethos. If I've learned anything, it's that acceptance is the key to so much, and we find so much freedom in feeling fierce about what we're accepting. (One big exception to this philosophy would be if you're dealing with something like gender dysphoria. There's also so much freedom to be found in owning your truth about what needs to be changed on your outside to reflect your insides!)

For the second exercise, we had to do a "show and tell" thing. I had planned to do yoga, but I didn't realize that we were going to be mic'd and on camera, which wouldn't quite work. I realized that my Züca bag, which I used for shoots and styling people on the go, was in the trunk of my car. All the other contestants were forming little groups in the green room and mingling each other to death. But despite that note about not being a wallflower, I knew that with the way that I am and the level to which I'd need to be able to serve all out in this setting, I needed to stay inside myself and not burn up all my energy in the off-camera green room. I knew because of so many failed attempts and different chemistry auditions I'd been on previously, it was important for me to stay focused on the goal and not let the other boys' posturing and peacocking derail me from my focus. I was Morgan Hurd in the 2017 World Gymnastics Championships. All eyes were on Ragan Smith to take all-around gold, giving America its would-be seventh consecutive individual all-around title, but she sprained her ankle warming up, so it all came down to Morgan to keep our hopes alive. I was Morgan Hurd, headed into the most intense competition of my career.

I digress.

So I went out with my bag and introduced her to the producers. "She's my little setcase," I said. "She and I have been together forever. She makes space for me for whatever I need, wherever I go. She puts up with me and she's doubly reinforced to put up with my big gay body. I can even turn her into a stool!" It was like the dry run of a stand-up act.

That night, they called and told us that half of us were going to be cut. I was stunned—they had flown in so many people from all over the place! The next day, we were down to twenty-five. I was shocked that I'd made the cut. Turned out they weren't fucking around in this Glendale Embassy Suites.

This might be surprising, but I really am an introverted stoner at heart: When I'm on, I'm on, but at some point I do need to recharge and plug in and just be with myself. Actually spending time alone with myself at night after giving all my energy to clients day in and day out was something I grew to need. But it also came as part of realizing that I'm a smart, kind, funny, hardworking, opinionated bad bitch with something to say. Being at the precipice of such a huge opportunity was terrifying and exciting. Would this reboot translate? If I book this, will it succeed? Will it be a flop and end my career? Could I even rise above these queens to get it in the first place? And was I sure I was *ready*?

But I wanted this show. As soon as I heard that tagline—that the show was about turning red states pink, one makeover at a time—it resonated. Quincy went two-to-one for Trump. Having been brought up in such a conservative FOX News-esque enclave, I knew I'd be able to maintain my spirit, and my cool, while also sorting out that FOX News outrage with gorgeous calm-and-collected facts.

That's what I tried to bring to the second day of auditions. I was still being funny, but I would wait for everyone to talk, then try to sweep in with some gorgeous knowledge. They started pairing us up in groups of five, and we would look at pictures of stuff that was in our vertical. Then it was our job to figure out what to say about it.

Gays started dropping like flies. You'd get attached to someone, and then they'd be gone. Soon we were down to fifteen people.

When we came back from lunch, we were doing our first-ever dossier reads—reacting to specific things from the files they'd prepared for us—on camera. There were some important people in the room by that point, and some other important people sitting in video village, where the people watching what was happening on camera were. People were rotating in and out, murmuring to one another between takes while we would all be sitting on these chairs in front of people, assuring ourselves this was all a completely normal experience, and at least for me, trying not to let the heartburn run down and explode out of my butt.

I knew who my biggest competition was: some fucking hairstylist, I mean a very nice boy, who didn't even have to come to the first day of auditions because he was already working on another successful unscripted TV show. All the gays whispered about him: "He's totally gonna be the one."

When they started rotating us into smaller groups, they called his name first out of all the groomers. There were only three groomers left. Then, not long after, they called me in and sent him back.

Only once I came in, I never left the room again. They kept moving other people around into different configurations but they included me. I was nailing this long program.

Either I'm booking this, I thought, *or they feel so bad for me that they're just letting me wear myself out because they're, like, Oh, poor queen, he's never gotten this far before, he thinks he's doing a little show! Let her do some stand-up and have a good time.*

At some point, the creator of the show stepped up to us and said, "You guys are five of the top ten."

Honest to God, my trachea fell out of my body onto the tip of my penis.

Then we went and got in two cars—split into two groups. They filmed us in the car driving to this gorgeous house and doing a lil episode beginning run-through. When we arrived, we split off into the house and began to do what we imagined we would do in an actual episode.

I found aromatherapy oil and started to do a sensory journey in the bathroom, including a wellness hand massage and a breathing exercise. "It's not about what the products are so much as how you feel," I told my pretend hero. "That's how self-care starts—you take care of yourself from the inside out. How much water you drink is as important as the moisturizer you use. And yes! I love this chest hair. Maybe we could trim it biannually so it's a little less of a thicket."

My car also had Karamo, Bobby, and Tan. But Antoni was in the other car. Our food guy was someone else entirely.

Every time I was on camera at the same time as Antoni, I had to stop myself from making weird faces, just from staring at him. *Girl, that sounds so good*, I'd think, and I would turn into Winona Ryder watching her *Stranger Things* costar accept their SAG Award.

I was personally hoping Antoni would get because I could listen to him talk about food all day.

Not long after, the five of us got the call that we had been cast. *Oh my God*, I thought. *I gotta move to Atlanta*. I was making a good living through my salon. I had come back to LA to become a successful, self-supporting hairdresser. I accomplished that goal. I faced down so many of my demons and came out on top. I felt like I was America's Next Top Model in the competition of my life. But this was a terribly exciting opportunity that I was so ready to launch into with everything I had. She was ready to go.

When the five of us descended upon Atlanta, I really didn't know what to expect. I'd never been there outside of the airport and had never spent a lot of time in the South. But I was really excited to get to spend more time with the boys and find out what it would be like to work on the show.

Bobby got there before us, because he knew the nature of his job takes a little longer to produce, so he spent more time on the ground before the rest of us arrived. But once we all got there, we really quickly seemed to fall into a good working space. We all went out together, the cast and crew, for the first time to practice some shot-blocking, where we should stand, to get an idea where to position ourselves in houses based on how much light and space we had to work with.

You may know that a lot of reality TV requires a lot of re-shoots, so the subjects have to deliver moments of emotion or vulnerability that may not have been caught on camera the first time. The team behind *Queer Eye* wanted to do our best to create moments of authenticity and connection the first time, so they wouldn't be reshot in a way that wasn't true to the way these moments unfolded. That's part of why I think the show has been received the way it is. It really is a natural depiction of events that aren't manufactured in the ways that we're used to having makeover shows manufactured. For me, having had a little bit of experience with *Gay of Thrones* up to this point, and just from watching TV, I knew this was an energetic, honest, and earnest attempt at connection that I don't know if I had seen done in this way before. We were all really inspired working together, knowing that we were creating something that was hopefully going to do some good in the world.

In my experience post-*Queer Eye*, I have fielded a lot of nervous-eyed questions about how true our onscreen connection is off camera. I get it. I've met a lot of celebrities in my time as a hairdresser who I anxiously hoped would live up to the idea of them that I had in my head, especially their relationships with their costars on TV. But the five of us really do love one another as much as it looks on the show.

That doesn't mean we didn't have growing pains. There were times, as in any family, where a few members spent more time together with each other than with others. But like with my actual brothers—the ones I grew up with—I feel well within my rights to talk about how maybe they have rubbed me the wrong way. But if I catch wind that someone outside of my family is talking shit about one of my brothers, you better hold on to your hats, ladies, because I am coming to you with the almighty force of Tyra Banks when she had to yell at Tiffany. "We were all rooting for you! Never in my life have I yelled at a girl like this!"

Bobby runs really hot. Karamo runs really cold. Like literally with temperature. I'm twelve minutes late everywhere I go and have zero personal boundaries. Tan is very boundaried and only five minutes late everywhere he goes. Antoni is the easiest, most laid-back guy. We all come together and gel, because at the end of the day, we all want what's best for each other. And there's not one thing about my sisters I would change in a million years. I love them so much and there's nobody else I could imagine going on this ride with.

When we moved to Atlanta, we actually shot seasons one and two together concurrently. For the first eight weeks, I was living in Atlanta but every weekend I would fly to Los Angeles or New York to maintain the clienteles I had built in both cities. At that point, I didn't know how successful the show would be. I didn't know if I would even keep doing hair after the show came out. I hoped I would, because I loved doing it.

But my good old busy bee part was right there for me, because I was not going to let my clients who I had worked so hard for so long to build up go without me. I didn't want to rely on this show for providing me with the rest of my life. I knew nothing in entertainment is guaranteed, and I couldn't abandon the career I'd already built.

Through the back half of shooting, I was introduced to a new part of myself I had not yet known: my powerful, bad-bitch corporate lady ferosh who wasn't afraid to kick ass, take names, and get shit done. Prior to *Queer Eye*, I was pining for a world where I could fully realize a life in entertainment and doing hair. Now, honey, my dream had come true. I was on camera Monday through Friday, flying to LA on Saturday, doing clients, shooting *Gay of Thrones* in its totality on Sunday, then back to Atlanta for my Monday-to-Friday grind as soon as I was done. It was fantastic. Was I stressed? Yes. Did my insides feel a little bit like I was being electrocuted? Yes. But like I learned in hair school: Fake it till you make it and make it look graceful. And that, I did.

Right up until episode fifteen out of sixteen, which was the firefighter episode.

A few producers and I had grown to love popping up on Bobby's field trips to prank him. I scared the bejesus out of Bobby twice on two of those field trips, and I knew he was scheming on a way to get me back. (The only person who feels worse about what happened than me is Bobby Berk, and he's given me full permission to tell this story.)

During the episode with the firemen, while Antoni and I had been applying my gorgeous egg-white-peach face mask, one of the firefighters stopped and called me over to look at one of the fire trucks. As I was looking at the instruments on the truck and trying to sort out what he wanted me to see, Bobby suddenly shot out from under the fire truck on a metal dolly with little wheels. He was trying to give me the fright of a lifetime, honey, so he grabbed my ankles. He was serving me *Scary Movie 2* eleganza.

I was wearing fierce gladiator sandals—obviously—and as he grabbed me, I felt this blinding white light that illuminated from my toe all the way up, but the dolly was covering my foot so I couldn't see what had actually happened. (My view was also obstructed by Bobby wiggling around making noises in jubilant joy, because he was so happy he'd finally gotten me back after so many pranks that he'd endured.)

"Bobby," I said, "stop moving. I think you just crushed my foot."

His face changed. "Oh my God, are you serious?"

"Yes," I said. "Stop moving! Get off!"

When he got up and I moved the dolly off my foot, my big toenail was lifted up like an open garage door. Like, my big toenail was past perpendicular to the ground. Like, about a 135-degree angle, if you're a mathematician. (I was only good at geometry, so if that visual escapes you, sorry!) There wasn't instantly blood everywhere, but as I hobbled as quickly as my grievously injured gay body could take me to video village behind those lockers, where the producers were, pools of blood followed me in every footstep. I didn't know how I was even going to unstrap this gladiator sandal to get it off me.

Coincidentally, my mom had picked this day of all days to visit set for the very first time. Thank God for her. She knew instantly that I was concerned about people touching me because of my HIV status—not that I would have been contagious, but it was something I didn't want to have to tell anyone about—and I live in fear of getting some kind of weird medication-resistant-staph-infection journey. It was one of the best times I've seen her be a true mama bear. She just cleared everyone away and ensured my personal space and made me feel as safe as possible in this very random situation.

And then I actually puked. Like full-blown threw up from blinding pain into a garbage can, and I was pouring sweat and shaking and trying to remove the gladiator sandal without touching the nail.

"Eight of you!" I roared, like an injured animal as a gaggle of very shocked firemen clamored to help clean up my mangled, bloody foot. "Eight of you thought this was a good idea! Nobody thought to look at what shoes she was wearing!"

One producer, who hadn't seen it yet, came up to me. "Come on, Jonathan," he was saying. "How bad could it be?" Then he saw it. "Holy fuck!" he yelled. Then he ran away to go throw up too.

As I was sitting in the chair, continuing to roar and make a scene, my mom leaned in and whispered in my ear: "You have a really good opportunity here to come off looking very normal. Very professional. You're starting to go off the rails from that right now. Let's pull it back. Why don't I just take you home?"

I popped my head up and realized she was totally right. "I would like to go home," I finally said. "I just need to go home. Mommy's in too much physical pain." So with the grace and poise of a Kerri Strug, I collected myself, hobbled out, filmed a usable button to end the scene, and went on home.

By the time I got home, I was feeling really bad for Bobby. It had been his birthday and I knew he was feeling completely terrible because never in a million years did he ever mean for me to be injured. And for the last two weeks of production, he and Tan and Antoni and Karamo carried every bag for me as I hobbled through the sets. The boys did their best to help make sure that I could do everything I needed to do.

But if you take a second peep at Mama Tammye's episode (how much do we love her, by the way), which was the next one we filmed after the firefighter episode, you'll see that I'm always in flip-flops with my big toe wrapped in a bandage. Because I could not even get my swollen-ass toe in a shoe.

And Bobby and I came out of that as sisters more than ever. I love you to pieces, Bobbers. If our friendship can survive a ripped-off toenail, our friendship can survive anything.

We wrapped our time in Atlanta at the end of the summer and I went for a gorgeous end-of-summer Fire Island moment and then went back to LA for business as usual as I picked up where I left off and continued doing hair five days a week: six weeks in LA, then two weeks in New York, as I'd been doing prior to *Queer Eye*.

That December, Netflix announced that the show would be coming out February 7, 2018. And I had no idea really what to expect. I knew that the salon had always been my safe place and the place where I felt the most engaged and the most needed and in my creative power, so I threw myself full force back into that and kept doing what I knew I could do best. I just waited for February 7 to come like it was Christmas. I was really hoping that by the end of 2018, I would, with some luck and by the grace of God, pass the 100K mark on Instagram. Little did I know that I was going to be left wigless from the *Queer Eye* makeover that our socials got.

On February 7, the day before the opening ceremonies of the 2018 Winter Games, *Queer Eye* premiered. Also coincidentally—in the long tradition of people dying on auspicious days in my family—Noonie's husband, Papa, my dad's dad, died the same morning *Queer Eye* came out. One of the last things he was lucid enough to see was our billboard in Times Square. He'd told me when I was seven years old that he knew someday I would be famous. He was also ninety-two by the time he died and very ready to bounce out of here, so it was as happy a passing as you can ask for. I knew he would have said the show had to go on, and so it did.

My life felt markedly changed. The show had been out for about a week. Mirai Nagasu threw her triple axel successfully and helped secure Team USA a bronze medal in the team figure-skating event in the 2018 PyeongChang Winter Games. And my in-box was starting to get flooded with notes telling me how my presence on *Queer Eye* was giving people a confidence that they didn't know they had. I realized that it was time for me to take some of my own advice and try something that I had always wanted to do. Years earlier, during the second season of *Gay of Thrones*, we'd had the opportunity to work with Margaret Cho, who was someone I'd already admired, both for her comedy and for her LGBTQ+ advocacy. After filming together, she said: "You should really be doing stand-up." It bowled my gay body over.

"Girl," I said, "you're a legend. I can't do stand-up. But I would live to do your hair, if you're not already attached to someone!"

Margaret being the queen she is took me on as her main hair chick, and after those years of working with Margaret, shooting *Gay of Thrones*, and now putting out *Queer Eye*, I was ready to take on a new challenge. So I decided that, after having done a few stand-up and storytelling events, I was ready to take my comedy aspirations out into the open. I did my first couple of sets between Los Angeles and New York with the full support of the *Queer Eye* boys in attendance.

In April of that year, I made another decision that would change my trajectory. After *Queer Eye* launched in February, by April I was at half a million followers on Instagram and my podcast *Getting Curious* had cracked the Top 10 on the iTunes podcast charts. But I was still doing hair five days a week and deep in credit card debt so I could pay my publicist. I'd been with an agency that, through the entire launch of *Queer Eye*, hadn't reached out for a meeting or shown any interest in my future. I made the decision to switch teams and start working with a different agency.

Listen: It's always hard for me to do that kind of thing because of her loyal-tea. But I had learned this lesson before, and this time I took care of it faster. If you're on a team that's not as passionate about your path as you are, then, queen, no harm no foul but you gotta go. And go I did to a team that changed my career forever.

No longer was I in the salon full-time. Now I was full-time producing my podcast, doing brand deals, performing stand-up, and ultimately going on press for the second season of *Queer Eye*. By this point, my life was an all-out transformation of her own.

Most of my twenties I was focused on survival or self-destruction. I worked hard to get through the turbulence caused by my childhood, and I had come out stronger, smarter, and developed the tools to self-soothe and grow. Now I was ready to help others do the same. To have the opportunity to be able to do things for other people, to try to be my best authentic self and have that resonate in a way that inspires self-acceptance in others, was blowing my mind on a minute-to-minute basis. I brought my mom out to New York. It was her first time being there as an adult, and I wanted her to have an authentic experience, so I took her down to the subway. That was my first mistake.

God love her, my mom hadn't been on the subway since she was fifteen years old and on vacation in London. Riding the train, she made deep, intense eye contact with every stranger there. Finally, a really sweet girl befriended us and realized that my mom's unyielding gaze was that of a midwesterner and not a murderer. She distracted my mom in conversation until we got off at our stop.

As a surprise, I got us really great tickets to go see *Hamilton*. But I had a really severe case of my biannual bong-chitis, which cold temperatures have a way of really exacerbating. I had one of those coughs that rattled through my entire body, and I was just trying to stifle it, but it was coming out every ninety seconds for the entire first act. Hot tears were streaming down my face—not because of the actors' incredible performances, but because I was so embarrassed.

Finally, the guy in front of me handed me a Ricola cough drop. "I love your show!" he whispered. It was one of those moments where I realized that my life had really changed.

In the second act, I was crying from a devastating turn of events. (I won't spoil it for you if you haven't seen the show yet.) I could feel my mom's little shoulders shrugging, too, and I turned to look at her, expecting to see her sobbing just like I was. But instead, she was laughing at me, because I was crying so intensely.

My mom has always been full of surprises. One time she sent me back a box full of all the gorgeous presents I'd ever made for her. I thought it was a slap in the face, but it turned out she was just decluttering her basement. Totally savage.

A few years ago, she learned to quilt. For Christmas, she had the nerve to make my two little nephews these really fierce baby blanket quilts. Meanwhile, she got me a gift card. Rude. How could she make a precious handmade gift for toddlers who barely even know her? I wasn't sure how my brothers weren't filled with this jealousy, so I very aggressively joked to my mom about how badly I needed a quilt for my thirty-first birthday.

I asked if she would make me one with some of my favorite power ladies on it. And so she went to Expressions by Christine in Quincy and printed out photos of all my favorite girls and made me a quilt with the following women on it: Aly Raisman, Simone Biles, Sarah Jessica Parker, Michelle Kwan, Michelle Obama, Midori Ito, Venus and Serena, Tonya Harding, Shannon Miller, Rue McClanahan, the cast of the *First Wives Club*, Princess Diana, Kerri Strug, Tara Lipinski, my grandma, herself (my mom), Julia Roberts, Reba McEntire, Nancy Kerrigan, Beyoncé, Whitney Houston, Madeleine Albright, and the Dixie Chicks. I love that quilt—it's on my bed. See, Mom, I totally use it.

* * *

Queer Eye's success has allowed me to have opportunities that are beyond my wildest dreams. It's more than I ever could have imagined would happen to me. And as amazing as those experiences are, having that many eyeballs on you and having your life and your career change that quickly brings on a new set of challenges and pressures and expectations, all of which have become factors in my life that I've tried to incorporate with grace and ease. But I do tend to struggle with popping the fuck off on social media. Sometimes my replies get a little hot-and-salty on ya. But I do the best I can because I'm still the same Jonathan that I was before I became famous. And I still have the same quick and inquisitive mind that has a lot of opinions. But I'm learning that with this amplified voice, those popping-off moments can be hurtful for the person I clap back to. Some days are easier than others, but I'm always trying to learn and do my best.

One thing that bothers me is when people only want me to be one thing: this effervescent, gregarious majestic center-part-blow-dry cotton-candy figure-skating queen who wants to give you feedback on your eyebrows and compliment your haircut. I am that queen a lot of the time. But that's not all of me. Sometimes I need to tweet about how we shouldn't be lionizing Ronald Reagan when he has the blood of countless gay men on his hands. That's when people tweet at me: "Can't you leave politics out of it? What happened to my sweet JVN?" Those people have probably thrown this book down and burned it by this point, though.

Things have changed in other ways for me, too, since *Queer Eye* came out. In love and dating, I was already kind of a nuanced package. She had her own list of baggage coming into any relationship. Add millions of eyeballs to your already nuanced package and dating life just became that much more complicated. Never before have I had to wonder if someone loved me for me or for the opportunities that my newfound success could bring in their life too. That's an extremely painful lesson. But like every other lesson I've had to learn, I can transform those times of deep hurt and find an opportunity to love myself and forgive myself more deeply than I knew I could. I may have had to soak a couple pillowcases through it, but, honey, I guess I really am a Kelly Clarkson song.

What I'm really saying here is, being flexible with myself through the ebbs and flows of what life has brought me has been really important. As things shifted and changed in my life, I've had different needs. Sometimes I've convinced myself that I'm not able to be anything that I need in and of myself, so I've reached out for other things that can end up doing more harm than they do good. If I recognize that no matter how much my life changes I am enough, and I am loved in and of myself and by myself, I'll be good.

Have you ever heard the adage that fame doesn't change

you—it just makes you more of who you are? My growing profile has made me even more loving and naively trusting, even when I shouldn't share that much of myself. She's working on it. And yet, I can't resist showing all of myself in interviews or on social media—even when that means showing my anger or flaws. I might look like sixteenth-century Jesus, but I sometimes struggle with being the landlord of Petty Lane, and I still operate like I have the audience that I did in 2010, which carries with it a different responsibility. Sometimes I look back and wish I had waited a bit longer before posting this tweet or that post. Being gentle with myself when I fuck up helps. My default is to be really critical of myself, but the world will do that for me, so I gotta make sure I always know I have my back. In general, if you can't take me at my raw, heated moment, you don't deserve me at my composed Emmys glam moment.

I love taking selfies with people. I love meeting people and hearing their stories. It's amazing. But sometimes I'm already twenty minutes late to an appointment with my doctor. Literally. And as I'm running late, I see someone beeline across the street with their phone out, and they have that look in their eyes that tells me I know they want to spill their story, and I have to say, "Girl, you're going to have to hit a hard U-turn and walk to this appointment with me if you want to chat," and half the time the initial reaction is, "Ew," because they think I'm being rude, but really I'm late to my doctor appointment, or the vet, or work.

Over the years I've heard horror stories of celebrities being dicks to nice people, and I always thought that was horrifying—why wouldn't you be nice to your fans? What did you think you were getting into? But what I've realized is that you can't be the same version of yourself at all times. Maybe your kidney function test results came back weird, so you have to go back to the doctor and you're worried, but you can't explain that to the fan who just wants a selfie. Maybe you just held your thirteen-year-old cat in your arms as they took their last breath, but the group of people wanting a picture don't care—they want their bubbly JVN, and they want him right now. It's been the honor of a lifetime to be held to this ideal, but what I really want to tell the people asking for photos is: I'm literally just as lost as you. I'm just as grateful. And I'm just as much of a perfectly imperfect mess. People are all layered—good and bad, filled with joy and sorrow. The key is being grounded in the relationship you have with yourself. Basing my worth in how I treat myself despite how others treat me has been the key to my success—and I want that for you too.

And I never want to be rude. But I'm literally going somewhere! Sometimes I'm running late to a meeting where there's a whole big group of people with a lot of money riding on me being there. It used to be, if I was late for an appointment at the salon, that was skin off my client's nose and the rest of my clients for the day. Now if I'm late, I could cause a whole set to derail. I could waste thousands of dollars. I could derail a project that a lot of people worked so hard on because I rolled in late, even if it was to make someone happy. Negotiating the new pace of my schedule with being so recognizable is a good problem to have, but it's a way that my life has changed.

People think they know me based on what they saw on *Queer Eye*. But for that show, there's sixty hours of footage shot for each episode, which gets edited down into a forty-five-minute run time. I don't edit the show, so I don't get to show you all the different sides of me on *Queer Eye* that you might see on Instagram, which is different from the one on Twitter, which is different from the one in the salon, which is different from the one doing stand-up, which is different from the one eating donut holes in front of the TV. (Some things, thankfully, never change.)

The thought of being dismissive to a kind person or a huge fan leaves a taste in my mouth like I've eaten a family-size pack of brown cinnamon sugar Pop-Tarts and gone to bed without brushing my teeth. As I've experienced a large swell in my public profile, I've understood a little bit more about the difficulties of balancing my personal life with a public persona. Think about how you would feel if you just stepped from office to office to office and never got to hang up your on-call hat. It can make you not be your best self. I hope that in writing about this part of my experience, I don't leave that unflossed overnight

Pop-Tart feeling in your mouth, because I would never complain about what I have. All I'm trying to explain is that every person you look up to, in whatever field they're in, is still just a person, with their own insecurities, worries, selfishness, and endless well of love and forgiveness. Famous or not, people are all onions with many layers.

Which leads me back to the importance of your relationship with yourself. The media, celebrity comparison, and the beauty industry—these are all worth billions of dollars and cause people unspeakable pain and trauma. Knowing I don't have to take on everything I hear and read as a complete truth for myself is my greatest freedom. Because at the end of the day, all we can control is ourselves in the vast array of situations we may find ourselves in. Controlling others and their choices is impossible, try as I might, so being compassionate and loving with myself can soften those uncomfortable outcomes. That's true for everyone—celebrity or not. I didn't look in the mirror and like what I saw until this one split second when I was sixteen. It was fleeting and very short. I spent so much time agonizing over my stomach fat, my love handles, my chest, and never felt the beauty of what I had. Feeling stuck in that space for so long made it difficult to learn to love how I look. I've been so many different shapes and sizes and have had to learn to love them all. We have unfortunately had very narrow definitions of beauty crammed down our throats for a long time. There are endless sexy shapes, colors, forms, and kinds of people who deserve celebration. It's each one of our jobs to reject that comparison of what we think beauty is and realize we are the motherfucking beauty. What we see on the outside doesn't always reflect what is inside, and vice versa. The only thing that matters is keeping your facts straight about how worthy you are of your own acceptance and love. Confidence is more about having courage to say you don't always feel on and poppin'. You're like, *I'm not sure about how this outfit totally is working but damn it, I came to slay*. Because I'm just so grateful for this moment.

You may see me serving a thigh-high boot, or a slayed red-carpet look, or doing something fabulous on the 'gram, but I'm still the same Jonathan who has to check in on all of my parts and make sure we are all okay. That we aren't having that old voice that feels separated from everyone—not masculine enough, too feminine, too round, too loud—and let him know he is loved and valued. I asked you at the beginning of the book, would you still love me if you knew everything about me? I hope that you do. But even more, I hope sharing my story encourages people to be more aware and compassionate on issues that may not directly affect them and spread that compassion to more people who need it. I have come to learn, though, that the more you love and accept yourself, the less you need other people's approval. I never want my childlike spirit, my desire to learn and entertain, to change. I'm still the same Jonathan, except nowadays I get to sleep under the tender gaze of all the power queens from my mom's quilt.

Unless I'm having an intimate moment in the arms of another, in which case I take that quilt and put it down on the bench at the foot of my bed. It's creepy to make love with your mom and Sarah Jessica Parker watching.

ON THE ICE

MY TOES WERE FREEZING. MY KNEES WERE SHAKING WITH stage fright in a way that I've never experienced. Some part of my brain was screaming: *You can't do this! This isn't who you are!* The autotuned beats of Cher's 2002 smash "Song for the Lonely" began to play. I nervously clagged through my first pivot-and-jazz-hands-reach choreography. I knew that I had to step up my performance if this was going to be a success.

Anxiously, I bent into my knees as I turned my head to the right. A hand outstretched, ready to join mine in our next counts of choreography leading into our lunge sequence.

My eyes locked into her enchanting gaze. She gave me an encouraging smile.

That smile belonged to none other than the most decorated American figure skater of all time. Michelle Kwan.

We began our lunge sequence. Cher was cooing, "I've seen a strong man cry." The tempo built. "When heroes fall . . . !" she sang. At that moment, I went into my seamlessly choreographed fall onto the ice. I knew I only had about four counts to go before Michelle picked my enamored gay face up in her hands, defeated yet hopeful, in time to dust the ice off and hit a stunning two-foot spin right at the apex of that first booming chorus: "This is a song for the lonely!" To the delight of Eliotskovatava—my skating coach, choreographer, and basically long-lost sister—we went from my spin right on cue to our synchronized choreography, then into our footwork and waltz jump sequence, moving perfectly into the rose-throwing onto the ice.

It was at that moment that I realized I wasn't in a fever dream. I was working with someone who I've looked up to my whole life, who for some incredibly otherworldly reason, was now my friend, and who had agreed to help me make a video to launch my first international comedy tour.

This wasn't an acid trip. This was my life.

Sometimes I think about what it would be like to go back to Quincy, Illinois, and see little Jack, that part of myself who was bullied to the ends of his world. I would tell that sweet powdered-donut-obsessed little boy who was so desperate for any morsel of love or acceptance that the future had big things in store for him. That one day, he would get to create dances with Michelle Kwan. That he would be in a position to realize his lifelong dream of learning to figure-skate, leaving his carpet routines far behind. That he would sell out Radio City Music Hall in front of six thousand people screaming for him to do a floor routine of his own with a special Michelle Kwan cameo, and that his ass would do a standing back tuck at thirty-two, HONEY!

What would Jack have done? He would have sprouted wings, flown up to a building, jumped off, and landed on his feet unharmed. And then he would have sent adult me to rehab, because I was clearly on drugs and delusional.

I spent so much of my twenties pushing little Jack aside. Instead of nurturing that child, I tore him to pieces. I hurt myself even more with every chance I got. It wasn't until I had lost everything I thought I wanted that I realized being an adult wasn't about being "normal," or having a life that seems enviable to people from the outside. Being a fulfilled and successful adult has required accepting that I do have an inner child who was hurt and traumatized. It's my job as an adult to nurture him, alongside all the other parts of me that make me who I am.

I wanted to share my journey because we have all done things we never thought we could and been places we never thought we would go. Good and bad. As scary as this can be I want you to know no matter how broken you feel, and how seemingly unlikely it is, we are never too broken to heal. More than that, there will be people who love and accept you completely, and there will be people who do not. If you love and accept yourself all the way, no matter what, through thick and thin, then either way you will make it through. If my story helps younger LGBTQ+ people, then the fear of sharing my truth in this book is worth it.

It's not about meeting other people's expectations. For me, it's about evolving with all the parts of my experience authentically: the parts that make me beautiful, the parts that have me ordering too much food, saying yes too much, or wanting to chat your ear off about cat behavior. We are all a beautiful jumble of layers, parts, and mixtures of experiences, but my most important part, and in my opinion everyone's most valuable part, is the one that chooses self-love instead of self-harm in the grand sweeping ways but also the little ways every single day. Learning to parent yourself, with soothing compassionate love, forgiving yourself, and learning from all the decisions you made to get you to where you are—that's the key to being fulfilled. Learning to be the dream parent cheerleader to yourself. It's been in you the whole time. And no matter how down you get, you can always make a gorgeous recovery.

Skating with Michelle that day wasn't a dream, no matter what my eight-year-old self might have thought. This was my real life. And it was happening now.

* * *

"Were you nervous?" Michelle asked me as we were taking our skates off. *Queen, did you make me sob uncontrollably at the 2003 World Championships?*

"Oh my holy sweet Jesus fucking Christ of course I was," I said. "My gay heart!"

"It all worked out, though," she said.

"Yeah." And I could feel a smile spreading across my face. "It did."

ACKNOWLEDGMENTS

I would have never gotten a chance to write this book if not for the exhausting work done by my mom to raise me.

Bug the first, you taught me to care for something and I would've never been able to survive my twenties without you.

To the Fab Five, your love and support means the world. Tanny-bananny, Ant, Karamo love, and Bobbers, I love you so much.

To the team at HarperCollins, especially Hilary, thank you for helping me to tell my story.

Patty, thank you for your endless acceptance.

To my whole team—Julie and Rae, and the team at CAA—who believe in me and work so hard to help me succeed, thank you.

For giving me the biggest opportunity, David Collins and Scout Productions, Jenn Levy, Jennifer Lane and Rachelle Mendez, and the rest of the *Queer Eye* crew at Netflix and ITV—thank you so much, especially for all your love and support.

Sam Lansky, thanks for your guidance.

To all my friends and family, I love you and hope you're not too pissed off if you were in the book.

Love always,

Jonathan

RESOURCES

Planned Parenthood

Planned Parenthood is the nation's most trusted provider of vital reproductive health care, sex education, and information. While they are most well known for their women's health services, they provide services for people of all genders. These services include HIV testing, education, case management, and prevention.

www.plannedparenthood.org

800-230-PLAN

RAINN

RAINN (Rape, Abuse & Incest National Network) is the nation's largest anti-sexual violence organization. They carry out programs to prevent sexual violence, help survivors, and ensure that perpetrators are brought to justice. They operate a 24-hour hotline that automatically routes the caller to their nearest sexual assault service provider.

www.rainn.org

800-656-HOPE

Phoenix House

Phoenix House is passionate about healing individuals, families, and communities challenged by substance-use disorders and re-

lated mental health conditions. With ninety-seven programs nationally and a legacy spanning fifty years, they provide individualized, holistic drug and alcohol addiction treatment.
www.phoenixhouse.org
888-671-9392

The Trevor Project
The Trevor Project is the leading national organization providing crisis intervention and suicide prevention services to lesbian, gay, bisexual, transgender, queer, and questioning youth. They offer a national 24-hour, toll-free confidential suicide hotline.
www.thetrevorproject.org
866-488-7386

National Coalition of Anti-Violence Programs
National Coalition of Anti-Violence Programs is a coalition of programs that document and advocate for victims of anti-LGBT and anti-HIV/AIDS violence/harassment, domestic violence, sexual assault, police misconduct, and other forms of victimization. Their site has a list of local anti-violence programs and publications.
www.avp.org/ncavp
212-714-1141

Advocates for Youth
Advocates for Youth works with young people globally in their fight for sexual health, rights, and justice. Through their ECHO program, Advocates for Youth recruits, trains, and supports young people living with HIV to serve as leaders in the fight to end HIV stigma and criminalization.

www.advocatesforyouth.org
202-419-3420

GLSEN

GLSEN wants every student, in every school, to be valued and treated with respect, regardless of their sexual orientation, gender identity, or gender expression. They believe that all students deserve a safe and inclusive school environment where they can learn and grow.
www.glsen.org
212-727-0135

Peer Health Exchange

Peer Health Exchange empowers young people with the knowledge, skills, and resources they need to make healthy decisions. They do this by training college students to teach a skills-based health curriculum in under-resourced high schools across the country.
www.peerhealthexchange.org
415-684-1234

ASPCA

The ASPCA is a national leader in animal rescue and protection, working tirelessly to put an end to animal abuse and neglect. They have shelters across the country where you can adopt a loving pet companion.
www.aspca.org
888-666-2279

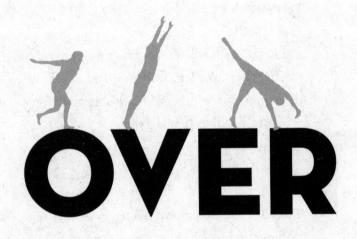

THE TOP